Formed in His Image

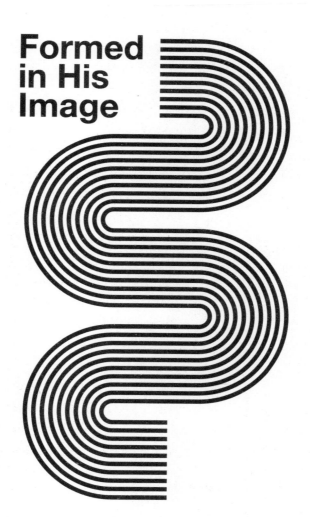

Formed in His Image

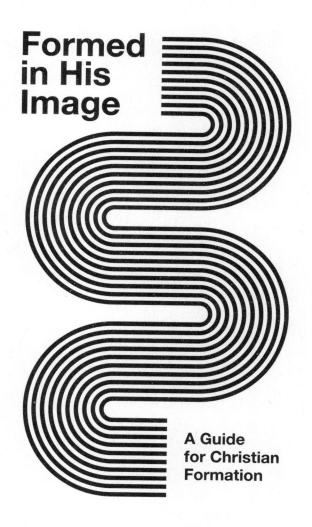

**A Guide
for Christian
Formation**

Coleman M. Ford

B&H
PUBLISHING
BRENTWOOD, TENNESSEE

Published by B&H Publishing Group
Brentwood, Tennessee

Dewey Decimal Classification: 248.84
Subject Heading: CHRISTIAN LIFE \ DISCIPLESHIP \
SPIRITUAL LIFE

Cover design by Micah Kandros Design.
Cover image by SunnyAfternoons/creativemarket.
Author photo by Angela Richardson.

1 2 3 4 5 6 • 27 26 25 24 23

Dedicated to my wife Alex who cares deeply
about spiritual formation and has been a constant
encouragement along the way.

Acknowledgments

Anne Dillard once wrote, "Putting a book together is interesting and exhilarating. It is sufficiently difficult and complex that it engages all your intelligence. It is life at its most free."[1] This process certainly has been interesting and exhilarating. Interesting because it allowed me to work out thoughts that I had previously taught on but needed to be explored in more depth. Exhilarating because it allowed me to rework those thoughts as if coming back to a painting once thought complete. And I'm not assuming its perfect by any means. It has been free because it has allowed me to connect different spiritual, emotional, and experiential life dots to a common theme. Difficult and complex because of the constant feeling of not knowing what to keep and what to throw out in the writing process (which is why we should love our editors). The freedom of writing is only so because it depends on many people to make it happen. In that way I have numerous people to thank. I must first thank Taylor Combs and then Mary

---

1. Anne Dillard, *The Writing Life* (New York: Harper Perennial, 2013), 11.

Wiley for allowing me the opportunity to work on this book with B&H. They took a chance on someone who had previously only written the occasional academic piece to engage a wider audience with his thoughts on spiritual formation. This was the first component of experiencing life at its most free. Along the way, many friends and colleagues provided insight and edits to my work. I am indebted to Todd Bates, Micah Carter, Matt Clakley, Garrison Griffith, Aaron Halstead, Philip Likens, Blake McKinney, Roy Onyebetor, and Shawn Wilhite for reading and commenting on various sections of the book. Thank you to my colleagues and friends at Texas Baptist College and Southwestern Baptist Theological Seminary for the opportunity to teach on these topics and work through them in my personal development and writing. Finally, I must thank my wife Alex who helped me work through concepts in the book, provided the necessary space for me to complete this project, and who continues to be a vital partner in formation. Everything that shines in this book is because of these lovely people. Anything that remains unpolished and opaque falls entirely upon my shoulders. May the glory of our triune God be magnified through this work so that the people of God may be more fully formed in the image of Christ for the sake of his Kingdom both now and forever.

Soli Deo gloria
Coleman M. Ford
October 2022

Contents

Foreword

P ractice makes perfect!" I was at Little League baseball practice the first time I can remember hearing that phrase. I was probably eight or nine years old, and I can still hear my coach yelling it from the dugout. Like any good coach, he was trying to instill the importance of grit, determination, and practice into a bunch of young baseball players.

He wanted us to learn how to keep our gloves down for ground balls and to use two hands to catch any pop fly that came our way. He wanted us to take a perfect practice swing in the batter's box before we stepped to the plate. The same phrase rang out, no matter what we were doing: "Practice makes perfect." Our coach understood a basic principle—performance in the game matches performance at practice.

Even as an eight- or nine-year-old, the phrase made perfect sense. The more you practice the better you get, and it proved true. The more our team practiced, the better we got.

The problem is, none of us ever became perfect, and the expectation of perfection can sometimes become overwhelming and discouraging. Every now and then a grounder would sneak below our gloves, a pop-fly would bounce out of our gloves, or we would strike-out, despite how many perfect practice swings we had taken.

Why should we keep practicing something if we are never going to perfect it? Over the course of time, many of us became too discouraged to continue. We were never going to be good enough. No matter how much we practiced, we would never be perfect.

Sometimes I wonder if Christians have a "practice makes perfect" mentality in their spiritual disciplines. We start every year with an annual Bible reading plan, convinced we will not miss a single day. We plan rhythms for evangelism, hoping to be faithful with every opportunity to share the gospel. We set aside days to fast and spend time with the Lord, sure that we will spend lots of time satisfied in the presence of God. But inevitably, life happens and we miss a day in our reading plan; we don't take the opportunity to share the gospel with our neighbors, or we forget about a planned fast and overwhelm and discouragement sneak in.

I believe, since you picked up this book, you need to hear this: your practice of spiritual formation will never be perfect, and it was never intended to be. Spiritual disciplines do not lead us to a perfect spirituality, they lead us to a perfect person—Jesus. The goal of your spiritual formation is all about progress towards the person of Christ.

In this book, you are not invited into spiritual perfection, but into spiritual practice that will lead you into a closer relationship with the triune God. My encouragement to you as you begin this journey is to reject a mindset of perfectionism and to embrace the idea that the goal is simply spiritual progress that will lead you closer to a person—Jesus.

J. T. English
Lead pastor of Storyline Fellowship in Arvada, Colorado, and author of *Deep Discipleship*

The Stories That Form Us

I'm a really big nerd. I like Star Trek. There, I said it. I like the science fiction genre in general, but I've always had a fascination with Star Trek in particular. Just ask my wife. She can't understand my affection for the Trek universe. From the classic series with James Kirk to *Star Trek: The Next Generation* featuring Jean-Luc Picard, and almost every other iteration, I'm a true Trekkie. One of my favorite series in the Star Trek universe is *Star Trek: Voyager*. The USS *Voyager*, captained by Kathryn Janeway (played by Kate Mulgrew), is catapulted into the Delta Quadrant, a distant and unexplored region of the galaxy. They are too far to simply warp their way back home in a few hours; in fact, they are over seventy years away from home at top speed. The crew of the starship *Voyager* includes a diverse group of people including Federation officers, former terrorists, a holographic doctor, and various new alien species. Not to mention they pick up a few Borg along the way. (If you know, you know.) The series includes the standard Trek tropes such as battles with hostile aliens, discovering new worlds, time travel, alternate universes, and a few cameos thrown in along the way (including an early Dwayne "The Rock" Johnson). But the point of the story is the journey home and the formation of the characters along the way. Each character has a story, from Tuvok the Vulcan security officer to Tom Paris the pilot with a past to B'Elanna Torres the half-Klingon engineer. Each story informs the larger story and contributes to the bigger narrative of returning home. This unlikely crew works against all odds to journey back to Earth, but they learn more about themselves and each other along the way. They must learn to trust each other, see the good in one another, and rely upon the gifts of others to accomplish their unlikely mission. Despite all odds, they finally succeed at returning to Earth as heroes.

I think this story is compelling for many reasons. For one, I think *Star Trek: Voyager* is a beautiful image of the church and Christian formation. No one would have put this group together intentionally, much like the church. Each character is challenged by their circumstances and peers to grow and be greater than they can imagine, as too are Christians in a community led by the Spirit. Each character is marked by the compelling mission to both explore in the name of the Federation, but also to return home to find peace and rest among loved ones. Christians are also shaped and formed by a mission, with the expectation of spending eternity at home with God. You don't have to be a Star Trek fan to appreciate a good tale of daring adventure and unlikely heroes rising to the occasion. In fact, this kind of story is present in much of the narratives we enjoy in books, television, and the big screen. In a sense, we see ourselves in these narratives. There is a bit of us in each of these tales. And if not, we want them to be true for us. We, in some small part, see stories such as these as part of our identity—or at least an identity that we long for.

We see this sort of story-driven identity emerge often in politics and social causes as well. A particular cause creates community and forges an identity. A story of identity is written, heroes are established, and icons are erected. Slogans, banners, and T-shirts are created. Social media hashtags are invented, and the formation of a people takes shape. The news is replete with multiple causes and the (sometimes rabid) supporters who stand behind them. They have been shaped by the story. The same is true for Christians. As believers in a crucified, resurrected, and reigning Savior, we have a cause—a Great Commission, you could say—to tell others the news of a different kingdom guided by different priorities ruled by a different King. We have an identity, one not written by social media influencers, but one imparted to us upon faith in Christ and sealed in baptism. This identity fundamentally reshapes who we are and what we are called to do in the world. We have a story, one found in the authoritative Scriptures, and one that gives us our Hero, as well as our cosmic enemy.

Christians are story-driven people just like the rest of the world. The difference is that ours is the true story of creation and the cosmos. It's the cause that makes the greatest sense. It's the charity that makes an eternal impact. It's the political position that transcends all others. It's the story of a God who created mankind, showed grace and mercy at our rebellion against him, and provided a way back to relationship with him through the all-sufficient atonement of the Son of God who took on flesh for our sake. We storm the gates of hell by the power of God's Spirit and God's Word under the banner held victoriously by a nail-pierced Savior. This is the story of Christian formation, and it needs to be the story that works itself all throughout the Christian life, from corporate worship to private devotion. It's the story of this book.

> **Christians are story-driven people.**

Going Straight for the Heart

I spent several years ministering to middle and high school students and their families. It was a unique time as it coincided with the rise of social media and the advent of the smartphone in the mid-to-late 2000s. I started in student ministry with a flip phone and ended as a fully engaged (and perhaps slightly addicted) smartphone user. I observed as my students became increasingly tethered to a phone, their social media accounts, and the ever-changing whims of a technologically advanced culture—and I was right there with them. We were being formed, yes, through Bible study and short-term mission trips, but also through an alluring vision of the Good Life presented to us on our glowing rectangles. The medium shaped the message as my ministry increasingly catered to technology and social media. I became an expert at crafting social media posts to highlight my ministry and attract students and their families. I made silly videos and posted them on YouTube.[1] While I don't think I ever reneged on biblical and theological fidelity, there were certainly times where successful ministry was gauged more by social media hits rather than gospel engagement. I didn't see then how easy it was for an alternate story, even one based on the good desire for ministry effectiveness, to creep in and take over. This is the power of stories. Stories shape our hearts, our desires, and lead us to act in certain ways. I'm not here to talk about the potentially damaging effects of smartphone or social media usage, but I mention this point in my own ministry to further illustrate how our formation as people, even in Christian contexts, can be misguided.[2]

We are all being formed in some way to believe, think, and act a certain way. From our families of origin, cultural expectations, political ideologies, and entertainment choices, there are many ways in which we are formed. Not all of this is bad. There is a God-glorifying reality in which our culture, language, and experiences are used for God's purposes. But there is also a sense in which we can be blinded to the less edifying ways these various forces shape our hearts and minds. Car and

---

1. I am not ashamed of silly youth ministry videos, by the way, and I am quite proud of the series I produced featuring a talking Mr. T plastic coin bank.

2. The effects of smartphone usage, social media engagement, and the like is well-attested in both secular as well as faith-based research. A book that has particularly helped me is Tony Reinke's *12 Ways Your Phone Is Changing You* (Wheaton, IL: Crossway, 2017). When teaching formation, I often refer to a *New Yorker* cover from 2015 that depicts a person bent over looking at the phone while missing the beauty of the world around them.

beer ads with wording like "Live the Dream" stir the heart and imagination. Billboards for home improvement stores get us to dream about what could be. Commercials for credit card companies present images of vacations and happy families. These sorts of images of living out your fantasies and wildest dreams are Marketing 101. And it works.

Whether it's a sports car, the latest energy drink, or cotton underwear, advertisers have learned the secret of getting into the hearts of consumers. It's more than information; it's formation at its most basic level. If you can get to the heart and imagination, you can get to the pocketbook. We all know the car will break down, the clothes will go out of style, and the smartphone will shatter or become obsolete next year. Yet we still give in to the well-crafted messaging. Most of us need a car, all of us need clothes, and smartphones have become indispensable for many of us. These objects are not inherently evil, but the way in which we perceive them in our hearts can be.

There was also another master of engaging hearts and imaginations. Jesus used numerous parables and illustrations to help his audience imagine what the kingdom of God is like. This was more than an exercise in information; it was a ministry of reformation. Many of his hearers were formed to expect a certain kind of messiah and to look for a specific version of God's kingdom, and they also had a certain view of themselves. They were shaped by a narrative, or perhaps a certain interpretation of a narrative, an interpretation that Jesus was there to correct. The Scriptures, the messianic promise, and the Kingdom all culminate on the person and work of

Jesus. To believe and trust in Jesus is to reorient one's view of the world and place in it according to the gospel. In doing so, we come to understand the different narratives that were once shaping us and clouding our vision to seek after what the apostle John calls the "lust of the flesh, the lust of the eyes, and the pride in one's possessions" (1 John 2:16).

You may be nodding your head and saying an internal "yes and amen." Evangelical Christians stand on the rich tradition of highlighting the need for rebirth by professing faith in Jesus Christ and living a life transformed by his grace and mercy. The problem comes in our response to the culture around us. When the culture offends the faith, we immediately go on the defensive. There will always be a need to defend the faith and emphasize orthodox Christian doctrine. But our typical response is too often to go straight to the intellect, piling on more Bible studies and longer sermons. We might even do a special training on apologetics. Rather than raising our shields against the culture and preparing our counterattacks on Twitter, perhaps we need to create grace-filled and mercy-laden gospel arrows aimed at the hearts of our own people. Rather than trying to cram more information into our brains, perhaps we need to engage the imagination and help others see God as more beautiful. One of the main tasks of gospel ministers is to regularly recapture

> The Scriptures, the messianic promise, and the Kingdom all culminate on the person and work of Jesus.

the imaginations of their people. The gospel is the better story to shape and fashion our lives in a world desperately in need of the hope of Christ. While this task should include addressing biblical illiteracy, doctrinal deficiencies, and the basics of spiritual disciplines, those good and worthy tasks will only be effective if we engage the heart and imagination. Only when we see formation as an exercise in love, not information, will our Christian life begin to flourish.

> **Only when we see formation as an exercise in love, not information, will our Christian life begin to flourish**

The Goal of Formation

Think of your favorite story. Think of the anticipation you felt in the rising action. Think of the peace you felt at the resolution of the crisis. Sauron/Voldemort/Thanos/Hans Gruber is defeated. Dwight finally becomes manager and Jim finds success in his dreams of sports marketing. Marty McFly successfully reunites his parents and rescues the time line. The starship *Voyager* finally reaches Earth. The gospel story is no different in this respect of resolution, though the plot of the story plays out on a cosmic stage. The story of the gospel is also different because we know the Enemy has been defeated. We merely live in the tension of the story awaiting final resolution in the coming of Christ in victory to usher in his kingdom in fullness. For Christian formation to be effective, we must maintain this story of the gospel at all points in discipleship. The story includes triumph, but it also includes trial and pain. The story is filled with the love and power of God, but also the schemes of Satan in the world. The gospel story has an end and purpose in mind, but we can easily forget that purpose. The gospel is *the* story of our formation. We are being shaped into the image of Christ, based on the person and work of Christ, for the purpose of making Christ known in the world, with the expectation that we will rule with Christ in a new heaven and new earth. This is more than a story of the guy finally getting the girl and settling down for the rest of their lives; this is a story of Christ fully redeeming his bride and unsettling the reign of death once and for all.

So, what is Christian formation? Here's the definition of Christian spiritual formation that will guide the remainder of this book: *The lifelong process of image-bearers called by the goodness of God, shaped by the truth of God, to behold the beauty of God.* I believe that this way of thinking about spiritual formation is helpful for us as we embark on the task of making disciples and promoting the work of the Spirit in the life of the church. This definition helps us understand the grand concepts of spiritual formation. First, this task is not a one-time event but a lifelong process. As we explore in this book, this is what Christian theologians call *sanctification*, and it's the continual process of the Spirit working in

> **Christian spiritual formation is the lifelong process of image-bearers called by the goodness of God, shaped by the truth of God, to behold the beauty of God.**

and through our lives. But we are all called to enter this process alongside the work and gifts of all members of Christ's body. Formation is Spirit-guided and empowered, but it is carried out by the ongoing and ordinary work of Christians seeking mutual growth in love for God and others.

Second, the church must unpack all the implications of being image-bearers of the triune God so that formation can be effective. We will consider the *imago dei* and the image-bearing qualities of humans, and what that means for our formation. We'll also unpack how union with Christ fulfills our image-bearing reality. Next, we are called into the story of the gospel by God. Paul reminded Titus: "But when the kindness of God our Savior and his love for mankind appeared, he saved us—not by works of righteousness that we had done, but according to his mercy—through the washing of regeneration and renewal by the Holy Spirit" (Titus 3:4–5). God's goodness to us in Christ provides shape to the Christian identity and the way in which Christians view themselves in the world. We have been rescued "from the domain of darkness" and transferred "into the kingdom of the Son he loves" (Col. 1:13). This is a total reorientation of our identity and reshaping of the way we think and act. This new story comes with it a new means of knowing what is truth; namely, God's Word. Thus, we are continually shaped by the truth of God. As we unpack this through the book, we must acknowledge that this means more than personal Bible study. Our formation is greatly impacted by personal study, but for formation to be meaningful, we need to be completely immersed in God's truth in a myriad of ways.

Finally, the entire point of our formation is so that we would experience the beauty of God both here and in the life to come. As we enter the story of the gospel, we begin to see the world for what it is: created as good by God yet marred by sin and in need of redemption. What previously attracted us no longer appeals to us, considering God's glory. As the hymnist Helen Howarth Lemmel once wrote: "And the things of earth will grow strangely dim, In the light of His glory and grace." We begin to see the true Beauty that all other beautiful things point us toward.

So this is the task of Christian spiritual formation. We are being formed in Christ's image for God's glory so we can experience his beauty. We will explore doctrinal foundations as well as practical foundations for formation to understand how this all takes place. For now, a fitting place for us to start is with the opening prayer found in Augustine's *Confessions*, written a decade after his conversion to Christ as he reflected on the work of God's grace in his life: "You stir man to take pleasure in praising you, because you have made us for yourself, and our heart is restless until it rests in you."[3] Let's begin exploring how Christian spiritual formation leads us to take pleasure and find rest in God.

---

3. Saint Augustine, *Confessions* 1.1.1 in *Confessions*, trans. Henry Chadwick (New York, NY: Oxford University Press, 1998), 3.

PART 1

Doctrinal Foundations for Christian Formation

CHAPTER 1

Beauty, Imagination, and the Good Life in Christian Formation

I have asked one thing from the LORD; it is what I desire:
to dwell in the house of the LORD all the days of my life,
gazing on the beauty of the LORD . . .
—PSALM 27:4

[The] vision we have of God or of the church or of the
good life—these pictures are where life makes up its mind.
—GENE EDWARD VEITH JR. AND
MATTHEW P. RISTUCCIA[1]

There is an itch that all of us need scratched. And no matter how hard we try, we can never quite reach it. We pick

---

1. Gene Edward Veith Jr. and Matthew P. Ristuccia, *Imagination Redeemed: Glorifying God with a Neglected Part of Your Mind* (Wheaton, IL: Crossway, 2014), 139.

up the newest gadget. Still itchy. We take delivery of the next generation SUV. Tingling still there. We look for the next housing development that promises an oasis for our family. Argh, still can't reach it. In our pursuit of happiness, there is always the prickling feeling that there is something more. If you still feel that itch, you are not alone. It's a longing that was never meant to be gratified by what we can buy, build, or borrow. It's a longing that was implanted in the hearts of mankind from the very beginning. This longing is part of the "restless heart" described by Augustine at the end of the last chapter. This famous line continues to resonate because it so perfectly captures the spiritual plight of mankind, as well as its antidote. Augustine's "restless heart" prayer can also inform our understanding of the Christian life and our ongoing formation. In fact, it is a thought that undergirds this entire book and gives shape to the thoughts and reflections proposed here. More than that, Scripture calls Christian disciples to desire and pursue the beauty of God, and by doing so, the Spirit reshapes and forms our imaginations toward a biblical vision of "the Good Life." This vision is the aim of Christian formation; namely, the beauty of God experienced in part in this life and in full in the life to come.

Why Beauty and Imagination?

We've lost the conversation on beauty and imagination in modern evangelical Christianity. We don't talk about the beauty of God today nearly as much as Christians did throughout church history. There are plenty of reasons for this, but primarily our western impulse for pragmatism and constant activity has shifted our attention from *being* to *doing*. We do not deny the existence of beauty and imagination, but we've lost the ability to speak about it meaningfully. We've lost the way in which beauty and the wonder of God relates to our Christian life and our journey with God. We've traded deeper theological conversations for the practical and pragmatic.

A focus on beauty requires a reorientation to the grander things of the world and our faith. Beauty deals with the very basic, yet profound, realities of God and redemption. Christians worship the Creator of all things, visible and invisible. We confess faith in a God who is Father, Son, and Spirit. We hold to the incarnation of the Son who took on flesh, died for our sins, and rose from the dead to redeem humanity and provide salvation to all who trust in the name of Jesus. We affirm the gift of the Holy Spirit to the church for sanctification and spiritual empowerment (see Rom. 6:19–22; 2 Thess. 2:13). We look forward to the return of Christ our Lord who will come to judge the living and dead and inaugurate his kingdom in fullness in a new heaven and new earth (see 1 Pet. 4:5). These are grand and magnificent declarations, full of grandeur and majesty. Paul speaks to the hope and majesty of the Christian faith in this way: "For our momentary light affliction is

> There are plenty of reasons for this, but primarily our western impulse for pragmatism and constant activity has shifted our attention from *being* to *doing*.

producing for us an absolutely incomparable eternal weight of glory. So we do not focus on what is seen, but on what is unseen. For what is seen is temporary, but what is unseen is eternal" (2 Cor. 4:17–18). Even to proclaim that God deserves all glory and honor is an affirmation of his beauty and transcendence above all other things.[2] And while we can capture these theological truths in creeds and confessions of faith and post them on a church website, the wonder of God is meant to engage our imaginations in holy and otherworldly sorts of ways. The glory, or beauty, of God is where true Christian formation begins.

> While we can capture these theological truths in creeds and confessions of faith and post them on a church website, the wonder of God is meant to engage our imaginations in holy and otherworldly sorts of ways.

But what about the imagination? Why focus on something so ethereal? Imagination is important because it is the way in which we make the connection between what we believe cognitively about God and what we do with our lives based on that belief. Some of you reading this may be dissuaded from seeing your imagination as beneficial for Christian spirituality. Some may even view the imagination

---

2. In the Old Testament, the Hebrew word for *glory* conveys the weightiness and splendor of God. The New Testament equivalent has a similar idea of otherworldly type of splendor.

as a gateway to sin and idolatry. It certainly can lead that direction, but it doesn't have to. Nor was it intended to. Gene Veith and Matthew Ristuccia, in their book *Imagination Redeemed: Glorifying God with a Neglected Part of Your Mind*, argue for the right place of the imagination in the Christian life. They say, "But just because the imagination can be the source of idolatry and other sins is no reason to ignore it. That the imagination can be used for evil means that Christians dare not ignore it. We must discipline, disciple, and sanctify our imaginations."[3]

Our desire for something greater, for beauty and significance, is primarily an exercise in the imagination. We imagine our lives feeling and looking a certain way. We arrange, in our minds, the family, the house, the community life, and the other things we desire in our hearts. The same is true with our spiritual life. We imagine where we want to be and how we want to grow, and therefore we begin to pursue those goals. Not only that, but the imagination is the place where we piece together the elements of the Christian life to build meaningful and beautiful lives. The imagination is the place where we encounter God in our minds. I'm not suggesting we engage in some form of soft idolatry, picturing God as an old man sitting in a rocking chair or Jesus as a blond-haired and blue-eyed bodybuilder. That's not what I mean by beholding God with our imagination. What I want us to consider is that we are guided in all other spheres of our life by our imagination, and our spiritual life is no less so. I believe this is part of what it means to love and honor the Lord our God with our minds (see Matt. 22:37). We grow, seek out new spiritual experiences,

---

3. Veith Jr. and Ristuccia, *Imagination Redeemed*, 16.

love others, and reach the lost with the gospel because, at some level, we first imagined it. Rather than being a roadblock to our spiritual formation, our imagination is the gateway.

The imagination, like every other part of our human experience, is subject to sin and the fall. While we should imagine good and holy things, we often fail to do so. We seek after false beauty with our hearts and minds. The apostle John speaks to this when he discusses the right and wrong kind of love: "Do not love the world or the things in the world. If anyone loves the world, the love of the Father is not in him. For everything in the world—the lust of the flesh, the lust of the eyes, and the pride in one's possessions—is not from the Father, but is from the world" (1 John 2:15–16). The direction of our love affects the outcome of our imagination. When the object of our love is God and his beauty, then our imagination follows suit. Indeed, the Spirit regenerates our hearts and continually illuminates our minds in this direction. When the object of our love is anything else, a devolved imagination comes with it. Our hearts and imaginations were meant to be captured by the beauty and majesty of the triune God. Anything less is a sham. This is what makes spiritual formation so necessary. In the corporate and individual practices of formation, we are in the process of constantly reshaping our imaginations to behold the beauty of God.

The Beatific Vision

Beauty and imagination within classic Christian thought collide in the affirmation of the Beatific Vision. The Beatific Vision, once commonly understood in Christian spiritual life, has been replaced with a vision of good marriages and families, health and wealth, or even consistent practices of spiritual disciplines in the Christian life. The pinnacle of Christian life is no longer the aim of beholding God in his infinite wonder and beauty. Losing the Beatific Vision in Christian spirituality removes both the majesty of eternity as well as the purpose for faithful Christian living in the present. We will dwell with God forever in a new heaven and new earth (see Rev. 21:1). Some thinkers in recent Christian history have attempted to direct the church back to this vision. Theologian Hans Boersma argues that the idea of the "vision of God" is a metaphor for the infinite otherworldly reality that will be our life with God. Though a metaphor, it is pervasive throughout Scripture to communicate our ultimate experience with God. Regarding the metaphor of vision in Scripture, Boersma states: "None of the [other] biblical metaphors . . . quite match that of vision. . . . No other metaphor implies the same thorough change in human beings, transfiguring them to be like God. And no other metaphor implies the same continuity of attachment to God."[4] When it comes to our eternal destiny, all we have are images and metaphors. While some images are clearer than others, they can only barely grasp the reality that will be beholding God's beauty and enjoying him forever. A related notion, the idea of the Good Life, is also something we need to recover for Christian formation to be effective.

---

4. Hans Boersma, *Seeing God: The Beatific Vision in Christian Tradition* (Grand Rapids, MI: Wm. B. Eerdmans Publishing, 2018), 5.

The Good Life

Everyone seeks beauty, and everyone exercises their imagination in the process. It's hardwired into our hearts to seek "the Good Life." Ancient philosophers such as Plato, Aristotle, and Epicurus all understood the Good Life and the ways you can have it. In his book, *Jesus the Great Philosopher*, biblical scholar Jonathan Pennington relays the importance of the Good Life in ancient thought and its usefulness still today. Pennington notes: "The Good Life is not referring to the lives of the rich and famous as revealed in a tabloid or exposé show. The Good Life refers to the habits of practiced wisdom that produce in the human soul deep and lasting flourishing."[5] The ancients understood that the heart is the core of our being, and that our actions are in some way connected. Certain virtues and habits contribute to one's practice and attainment of the Good Life. Biblical authors understood this as well.

Psalm 1 begins with the declaration: "How happy is the one who . . ." and follows with warnings not to walk in ways of wickedness and sin which lead to destruction—the literal opposite of happiness. The psalmist's prescription for happiness? To "delight [in] the LORD's instruction" and constantly meditate on the Lord and his Word (v. 2). The metaphor for happiness given in Psalm 1 is of one who is like a flourishing tree with ripe fruit, resistant to drought and decay. But compare this to the opening words of Ecclesiastes. Like a deep ominous voice-over in a dystopian action movie he states:

---

5. Jonathan T. Pennington, *Jesus the Great Philosopher: Rediscovering the Wisdom Needed for the Good Life* (Grand Rapids, MI: Brazos Press, 2020), 29.

"Absolute futility . . . Absolute futility. Everything is futile" (1:2). So, which is it? Can we be a flourishing tree of ultimate happiness, or is everything truly futile? I don't think these two observations contradict, but both serve to illustrate physical and spiritual realities of the human condition. The pursuit of things on earth, apart from a God-directed vision, is fruitless. It also speaks to the reality of sin which comes in and distorts the vision of the Good Life, replacing it with a vacuous vision of fleeting wealth, power, fame, and the like. Solomon knew all too well the vanishing nature of fame and wealth. These images describe how Scripture, particularly in the Wisdom literature, shows what the Good Life is all about. Jesus, too, spoke to aspirations of the Good Life.

The idea of the Good Life and human flourishing was central to Jesus's message of the kingdom of God. The Kingdom, however, is drastically different from any other vision of the Good Life. In another work by Jonathan Pennington, *The Sermon on the Mount and Human Flourishing*, he shows how the most famous teaching of Jesus should be interpreted with the lens of the Good Life in mind. Regarding the question of human happiness in Scripture, Pennington observes: "The Sermon [on the Mount] is not the only place in the New Testament or whole Bible that addresses this fundamental question. I would

> The idea of the Good Life and human flourishing was central to Jesus's message of the kingdom of God.

suggest that this question is at the core of the entire message of Scripture. But the Sermon is at the epicenter and, simultaneously, the forefront of Holy Scripture's answer."[6] The kingdom of God is where we will find true happiness, but the way we get there is through the unique practices of humble and sacrificial living and finding our identity in Christ.

> For spiritual formation to take root and thrive, we need to remember that God does care about our happiness, and only an abiding life in him will bring about the flourishing we all desire.

Jesus speaks similar "happiness" language with his disciples prior to his passion: "Remain in me, and I in you. Just as a branch is unable to produce fruit by itself unless it remains on the vine, neither can you unless you remain in me. I am the vine; you are the branches. The one who remains in me and I in him produces much fruit, because you can do nothing without me" (John 15:4–5). Harkening back to Psalm 1, Jesus is clear that fruitful living is only possible in him. Flourishing takes place in union with Christ. Language of "abide" or "remain" and "joy" in the New Testament speak to this idea as well. We must remember that the Bible, indeed our Savior himself, is

---

6. Jonathan T. Pennington, *The Sermon on the Mount and Human Flourishing: A Theological Commentary* (Grand Rapids, MI: Baker Academic, 2017), 14.

concerned with true human happiness. For spiritual formation to take root and thrive, we need to remember that God does care about our happiness, and only an abiding life in him will bring about the flourishing we all desire.

Recovering Good, True, and Beautiful

We've already seen how beauty, the imagination, and the Good Life are central to the biblical story. Another aspect in need of recovery is the notion of the true and good alongside beauty. Collectively, these are known as the transcendentals, meaning the irreducible qualities of being. If this sounds strange to you, don't worry. While Plato and Aristotle spoke of these qualities, it was later Christian theology that sharpened their usage and applied them to the being of God. The transcendentals (goodness, truth, beauty) are ultimate qualities of our experience that culminate in God. God is goodness, truth, and beauty. James Bryan Smith observes: "Beauty, goodness and truth are like the Trinity, of one essence. When all three are aligned—beauty, goodness, and truth—you are dealing with reality at its deepest level."[7] Christian thinkers have also clarified our understanding of the transcendentals to understand that when one is present, they all are present. Therefore, if something is true it is also good and beautiful and so forth. Thus, Christian formation asserts that the only true, good, and beautiful life is found in Jesus Christ. When it comes to how to understand these concepts practically, this figure should help.

---

7. James Bryan Smith, *The Magnificent Story: Uncovering a Gospel of Beauty, Goodness & Truth* (Downers Grove, IL: IVP Books, 2017), 11.

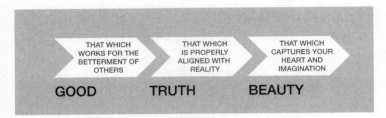

Figure 1. The Transcendentals

If you recall, the paradigm for formation in this book is the *lifelong process of image-bearers called by the goodness of God, shaped by the truth of God, to behold the beauty of God.* It is essential for us to recapture the language of goodness, truth, and beauty to live meaningful Christian lives. Let me briefly explain how each of these relates to our formation as believers.

Called by the Goodness of God

As I mentioned in the beginning, we are shaped and formed by different stories. Such narratives have the power to direct our hearts and actions. Even as Christians, it is easy for us to be led by a story other than the gospel. Therefore, our understanding of spiritual formation must start with the goodness of God, specifically the reality that he has called us into a different story. The story of formation is the story of the gospel. We are formed to be gospel people. Paul declares: "He has rescued us from the

> **It is essential for us to recapture the language of goodness, truth, and beauty to live meaningful Christian lives.**

domain of darkness and transferred us into the kingdom of the Son he loves. In him we have redemption, the forgiveness of sins" (Col. 1:13–14). Christian formation is based on the goodness of God, so that we would enjoy his goodness and enjoin others to "taste and see that the LORD is good" (Ps. 34:8). Formation, both corporately and individually, should never veer from the story of God's goodness to us in Christ. We must at every possibility emphasize God's goodness in making us a part of his family through Christ. We celebrate what the apostle Peter declares: "Once you were not a people, but now you are God's people; you had not received mercy, but now you have received mercy" (1 Pet. 2:10). God is truly good to his people, and this undergirds everything we pursue in our formation.

Shaped by the Truth of God

Truth is not just about facts, but it is woven into the fabric of reality. We need truth to build meaningful (i.e., good and beautiful) lives. Facts change; truth is eternal. It is a fact that it is currently 104 degrees in Texas while I write this, but later this evening it will be 88 degrees. These facts about the weather will change, and prayerfully, we'll see a cold front come through soon. Truth, on the other hand, relates to what is real about the world, ourselves, and God. God created all things visible and invisible, and he made us in his image. This is the truth. Additionally, Christ as the Word of God is the truth of God (see John 1:14–17; 14:6). Thus, spiritual formation can only take place when we emphasize God's truth at every turn. A truth or Word-centered spirituality is the only way that we will grow. It's the only way we will have good and beautiful lives. It's a tragedy when God's Word is neglected in the life of the church. We become less whole and more fractured as a people. Only the unified truth of God's Word can help us grow into the image of Christ. Christ prayed to the Father: "Sanctify them by the truth; your word is truth" (John 17:17). We need Scripture to saturate every aspect of our formation. From biblical preaching to biblical meditation, the truth of God shapes us into the life and character of Christ. God's truth continually affirms our identity in Christ and our mission for his kingdom. When we wander from the truth of God, our Christian formation fizzles and dies.

> When we wander from the truth of God, our Christian formation fizzles and dies.

Beholding the Beauty of God

Hopefully, you are starting to be convinced of the need to recover the language and idea of "beauty" in Christian spirituality. We can't talk about it enough. I believe it is *the* aim and focus of our formation. Beauty is powerful, captivating, and deeply affects us. Beauty also has the power to help us in trials. Paul says, "For our momentary light affliction is producing for us an absolutely incomparable eternal weight of glory. So we do not focus on what is seen, but on what is unseen. For what is seen is temporary, but what is unseen is eternal" (2 Cor. 4:17–18). The eternal weight of glory is the perpetual experience of God's beauty and majesty. Because God himself is beauty, he should be our sole focus and aim. All formation should be aimed at knowing and enjoying God in his manifest works in the world and salvation. Therefore, glorifying and enjoying God is the "chief end of man."[8] Beauty moves us, and the beauty of God is meant to move us the most. Anything that we consider beautiful is but just participating in God's beauty and infinite majesty. And while we may only have glimpses of his glory, the Beatific Vision discussed earlier affirms that we will perpetually experience his beauty for eternity. Truly, this is the only aim in life that matters.

But Why Goodness, Truth, and Beauty?

Why all this talk about goodness, truth, and beauty? Does it really matter? It might sound like ivory-tower philosophical talk, but it's quite practical. Though the concepts may be larger than life, they impact our daily lives in significant ways. This is because we live in a world that has completely neglected the transcendentals. In a modern world, we have lost a sense of the sacred. The notion of mystery is all but removed, and our experience is reason-driven rather than faith-driven. This is true for much of the church as well. Formation has devolved into doing rather than being. What we do is vital, but what

---

8. This comes from the first question of The Westminster Shorter Catechism, a seventeenth-century work based on the theology of the Westminster Assembly which met for the purpose of restructuring the English church. The Westminster Confession of Faith and catechisms are used in many reformed, particularly Presbyterian, churches today. The confessions and catechism were also influential on other traditions such as Anglicans and Baptists.

we do in our Christian life arises out of who we are and what
we believe. Both in the world and in the church, connection
between the daily and the divine is lacking.

We have also lost our sense of what it means to be emplaced.
To be human is to mean we corporeally exist in a certain loca-
tion at a certain time. The problem is our culture is always on
the move. We can be virtually anywhere with the tap of a
screen. Our physical existence is increasingly devalued while
our digital experience is continually prioritized. Theologian
Craig Bartholomew observes: "In our late-modern age we have
lost that very human sense of place amidst the time-space
compression characteristic of 'postmodernity' and globaliza-
tion. Place has become something that one moves through,
preferably at great speed, and virtual reality is no re-place-
ment."[9] In other words, we can determine our place rather than
our place determining us. This doesn't mean we shouldn't move
for a job or school, but Christians need to recover a sense of
place to be fully formed disciples of Christ. As we will see in
this book, corporate formation and understanding our mission
depends a lot on our place. God has called us to a place "for
such a time as this" (see Esther 4:14). Without a sense of place,
our formation is stifled. With a sense of place, we have a greater
sense of ourselves and our calling.

Last, we need to recover the notion of goodness, truth,
and beauty because we can easily lose gospel focus. The gospel message always takes us back to what is good, true, and
beautiful. It is easy for other desires and stories to infiltrate

---

9. Craig G. Bartholomew, *Where Mortals Dwell: A Christian View of
Place for Today* (Grand Rapids, MI: Baker Academic, 2011), 3.

our hearts. The gospel is not just a one-time decision, it's a life-shaping story. Without a gospel focus, discipleship and formation in the church will be weak and ineffective. As we will see with the means of grace in corporate and personal formation, the gospel is the focus of everything we do. Only the gospel makes us whole and flourishing

> **Only the gospel makes us whole and flourishing people, equipping us for life now and preparing us for life to come.**

people, equipping us for life now and preparing us for life to come.

Final Thoughts

While we may not use terms such as the Good Life, truth, goodness, or beauty in our everyday vocabulary, these ideas inform everything we think, feel, say, and do. The decisions you and I make are based in some small way on our vision of what human flourishing looks like. We all have a basic notion of what is good, true, and beautiful and act according to those impulses. Politicians, philosophers, advertisers, and talk show hosts all promote different versions of the Good Life. The desire for the Good Life is implicit within us because it is something woven into our hearts since Creation. We are never fully satisfied apart from life in Christ aimed at the beauty of God, to be realized eternally in the vision of God. With the idea of the Good Life in Christ, we can begin to build beautiful lives in the church and in our everyday lives. Only when we pursue what is good, true, and beautiful will our spiritual formation take shape and flourish in all the ways God intends for us.

Resources for Further Study

Jonathan T. Pennington. *Jesus the Great Philosopher: Rediscovering the Wisdom Needed for the Good Life.* Grand Rapids, MI: Brazos Press, 2020.

————. *The Sermon on the Mount and Human Flourishing: A Theological Commentary.* Grand Rapids, MI: Baker Academic, 2017.

Tim Savage. *Discovering the Good Life: The Surprising Riches Available in Christ.* Wheaton, IL: Crossway, 2019.

James Bryan Smith. *The Magnificent Story: Uncovering a Gospel of Beauty, Goodness & Truth.* Downers Grove, IL: IVP Books, 2017.

Gene Edward Veith Jr. and Matthew P. Ristuccia. *Imagination Redeemed: Glorifying God with a Neglected Part of Your Mind.* Wheaton, IL: Crossway, 2014.

Questions for Reflection

1. Is the idea of "beauty" or the "beauty of God" emphasized in your local church? If so, in what ways? If not, what do you think is the reason?

2. Why might the idea of the "Beatific Vision" in Christian spirituality not be attractive in modern culture? Modern evangelical church culture?

3. What are the common notions of the "Good Life" represented around you? In what ways do you feel like you have bought into competing visions of the Good Life?

4. If truth is the means of our formation, what ways can the truth of God be emphasized more in your life? We will cover this in more detail in chapters 5 and 6.

5. Take a moment to use your imagination and think about what a flourishing Christian life looks like to you. Write down what you imagine and begin praying over the ways in which those things may take root in your life.

CHAPTER 2

Getting the Trinity Right for Formation

To believe and love the Trinity is to possess
the key to all of theology.
—CHARLES SPURGEON[1]

The fact that we, who are made in God's image,
are invited into the trinitarian community is
the greatest invitation we could ever receive.
—JAMES BRYAN SMITH[2]

An ice cube. A three-leaf clover. An egg. A s'more. What do these have in common? They've all been used as

---

1. Sean Stone, "8 Spurgeon Quotes on the Trinity," Spurgeon.org, https://www.spurgeon.org/resource-library/blog-entries/8-spurgeon-quotes-on-the-trinity/.

2. James Bryan Smith, *The Magnificent Story: Uncovering a Gospel of Beauty, Goodness & Truth* (Downers Grove, IL: IVP Books, 2017), 48.

illustrations to describe God as Trinity. And every single one of them (including any others you might've heard in youth groups or on YouTube) are inadequate to describe the profound mystery and deep biblical reality of God as three-in-one. So, first things first, let's ditch the unhelpful analogies and simply choose to dwell in the richness and mystery of the Trinity. Only by doing so will we develop a true heart of worship, and a more faithful and robust Christian spiritual formation in the church.

Whether from a preschool playroom or a preacher's pulpit, the church's formational task is to imprint the reality of Father, Son, and Spirit in all of life. It is not an exaggeration that evangelical Christians either misunderstand God as Trinity or dismiss it altogether. I have found that most churches, whether in prayers, preaching, or praise songs, are functional Unitarians. They pray to God generally without understanding him specifically. I have no doubt that many such prayers are well-meaning and generally theologically sound as they are. But I want to submit to you that when we grow in our understanding of God as triune, everything from our prayer life to our personal relationships are enhanced. Though we may have a confession of faith in the Trinity, I believe that this confession does not often take root in the life of the church. The Trinity, however, is the lifeblood of Christian discipleship. Michael Reeves puts it this way: "No exaggeration: the knowledge of this God turns lives around."[3] Even small children can grasp the basic wonders of the triune God. On a regular basis

---

3. Michael Reeves, *Delighting in the Trinity: An Introduction to the Christian Faith* (Downers Grove, IL: IVP Academic, 2012), 10.

our home spends time in the New City Catechism. Modeled off older Protestant catechisms, one of the earliest questions states: "How many persons are there in God?" The basic answer is: "There are three persons in the one true and living God: the Father, the Son, and the Holy Spirit. . . ."[4]

The smartphone app for the New City Catechism provides an accompanying song for children. One morning my son repeatedly asked to hear the song. I reckon we listened to the song over a dozen times until I said we had to stop. I felt bad denying my son the thrill of learning basic Trinitarian doctrine, but it was time to move on with our day. What struck me was my son's basic joy in the song describing the Trinity. While my son can't explain different models of the Trinity (yet!) or fully plumb the depths of God's nature (who can?), he can appreciate the basic biblical foundations for the doctrine of God and find simple pleasure in singing about God as three-in-one. I trust that this foundation will grow and develop as my family and our local church continue to emphasize the Trinity as central to the Christian faith. Thus, the Trinity can and should be integrated into the Christian life from start to finish. But the question that faces the evangelical church today is whether our people have even a basic grasp of Trinitarian doctrine. The Trinity informs everything from our doctrine of salvation to the practical ways we understand community and fellowship in the local church.

So, what is the doctrine of God taught in our Sunday schools, youth groups, and worship songs? Do we walk away

---

4. Collin Hansen, ed. *The New City Catechism Devotional: God's Truth for our Hearts & Minds* (Wheaton, IL: Crossway, 2017), 25.

from Bible study and corporate worship with a greater sense of God as Father, Son, and Spirit, or do we walk away from church with a doctrine of God that is foreign to Scripture? It is not my goal to give you a full rendering of the Trinity, but rather help you see why we can't separate the Trinity from our spiritual lives and ongoing formation. The consequences for our formation are grave if we get the Trinity wrong. On a practical level, knowing that God is Trinity informs many elements of our formation. God is the aim and substance of our formation. If God is triune, then our formation must necessarily be communal in nature. Let's begin by exploring the basics of Trinitarian doctrine, then elaborate on how the Trinity connects to our spiritual formation.

> The Trinity can and should be integrated into the Christian life from start to finish.

Trinity 101: Biblical Foundations

The Bible clearly reveals that God is triune. Michael Reeves affirms: "To know the Trinity is to know God, an eternal and personal God of infinite beauty, interest and fascination. The Trinity is a God we can know, and forever grow to know better."[5] The triune God is the only one worthy of worship. The Trinity is a basic biblical truth and is something that the early church fought to maintain against those who taught false doctrine regarding the doctrine of God. In the following,

---

[5] Reeves, *Delighting in the Trinity*, 12.

I want to mark a few spots on the map of basic Christian Orthodoxy regarding the Trinity. It is true that the word *Trinity* is not in the Bible (as Mormons, Jehovah's Witnesses, and Unitarians are quick to point out), but you can't escape a plain reading of the Bible without emerging with this basic truth: there are three persons in one God. The entire Scriptures paint the picture of God as triune.

> **God is the aim and substance of our formation. If God is triune, then our formation must necessarily be communal in nature.**

Scripture provides specific "triadic passages" that elaborate the triune nature of God. For example, when speaking of God's love in Romans 5, Paul bases the love of the Father on the justifying work of Jesus Christ. That love has then been "poured out in our hearts through the Holy Spirit who was given to us" (v. 5). Paul concludes his second letter to the Corinthians with a brief exhortation: "The grace of the Lord Jesus Christ, and the love of God, and the fellowship of the Holy Spirit be with you all" (2 Cor. 13:13). All three persons are referenced in relation to God by the apostle John when he states: "Now this is his command: that we believe in the name of his Son, Jesus Christ, and love one another as he commanded us. The one who keeps his commands remains in him, and he in him. And the way we know that he remains in us is from the Spirit he has given us" (1 John 3:23–24). Besides these short passages, we see trinitarian imprints throughout other places in the New Testament. The writer of Hebrews discusses at length the relationship of the Son and Father and attributes divine personhood to the Spirit (for example, Heb. 1:2–3, 3:7). In the book of Revelation, John's vision reveals the culmination of redemption and describes Jesus sitting next to the throne of the Father (3:21) and the Spirit as speaking forth the words of God (14:13).

In the gospels, Jesus uses the language of sonship in reference to himself, as well as the language of Father in reference to his relationship as Son. The Spirit, present in the gospels, though prominent in places such as Acts, is described in personal and ontological ways. I will highlight the work of the Spirit more later, but suffice it to say, the Bible is replete with ways to describe the Trinity. The progressive revelation of Scripture demonstrates that glimpses of God's triune nature are given in the Old Testament, while the full revelation of God as Trinity is provided in the New Testament. To the disciples on the road to Emmaus, Jesus explained how all the Law and Prophets pointed to himself (Luke 24:25–27). In general, the New Testament writers help shed light on the way to read the Old Testament considering the revelation of Jesus the Christ and the gift of the Holy Spirit. From the Gospels to the writer of Hebrews to John's Apocalypse, the New Testament helps the church understand the Trinitarian "grammar" for describing God. This grammar has come to be known as "prosopological" and "partitive" exegesis. Prosopological exegesis (from the Latin *prosopon*, meaning "person") understands how to interpret each Person of the Godhead as described in Scripture. Partitive exegesis is related but focuses more upon the relationship between Christ's human and divine natures and how each is explained in Scripture. Each of these methods of understanding the way Scripture talks about the Trinity was developed and codified in the first centuries of the early church.[6]

Trinity 101: What Else?

When we oversimplify the Trinity, we get ourselves in trouble. Like the early church, we should read our Bibles like Trinitarians and take the Trinity seriously. We need to sing, preach, teach, and confess the Trinity and continually be shaped by the truth of the Trinity. Early heresies, however, sought to water down the mystery of the Trinity in various ways. Justin Holcomb describes a heretic as "someone who has compromised an essential doctrine and lost sight of who God really is, usually by oversimplification."[7] Oversimplification happens when we sacrifice the mystery of God and prioritize one or a few verses of Scripture to the neglect of the whole. The error of heresy is to evacuate the mystery and oversimplify the doctrine of the Trinity. We have seen how early Christians believed and demonstrated that the entire Bible shows the persons of the Godhead working in tandem with one another to accomplish the work of redemption. This is

---

6. To better understand how the early church read the Old Testament in a Trinitarian way, see Matthew W. Bates, *The Birth of the Trinity: Jesus, God, and Spirit in New Testament and Early Christian Interpretations of the Old Testament* (Oxford: Oxford University Press, 2016).

7. Justin S. Holcomb, *Know the Heretics* (Grand Rapids, MI: Zondervan, 2014), 11.

not "putting God in a box" but rather an attempt to be faithful to the revelation of God for the sake of the people of God. God's people need to understand who God is and how to relate to him. A basic understanding of Trinitarian doctrine should inform everything from the worship life of the church to the devotional life of the individual Christian. Let's explore basic Trinitarian doctrine a bit more before moving toward ways that the Trinity impacts our spiritual formation.

Christian orthodoxy maintains the threeness and oneness of God. We are not Unitarians, nor are we polytheists. What theologians call the "inseparable operations" of God simply means that no one person of the Godhead works independent of the other. On this point, theologian Christine Norton says, "When the Triune God acts outside of himself, he acts in a way consistent with his being— from the Father, through the Son, by the power of the Holy Spirit."[8] Where the Father is working so is the Son and the Spirit and vice versa. We also see that the Father, Son, and the Spirit are coeternal and coequal. All three are worthy of worship, praise, and honor. No one person of the Godhead is above the other, nor does one have more authority or exert a different will upon the other. Within the Godhead, there is mutual love and no subordination of one to the other. There is

> When we oversimplify the Trinity, we get ourselves in trouble.

---

8. Christine Norton, "The Trinity," *TGC Concise Theology*, https://www.thegospelcoalition.org/essay/the-trinity/ (accessed July 7, 2022).

one divine will. In the Incarnation, the Son assumed a human nature, including a human will, yet he is not less than the Father, nor eternally subordinate to him. What Paul describes in Philippians 2:8–10 is a beautiful expression of humility that does not deny Christ's full deity, but simply honors him for his work of taking on flesh and submitting himself to death for our sake. His submission is demonstrated in the Incarnation, not in his divine person. All these points, while appearing to be the trivial debates of theologians, impact Christian faith and practice significantly. To have a faulty and deficient view of the Trinity can—and often does—lead to faulty and deficient Christian practice.

The last point to make in our overview of Trinitarian doctrine is the triune God and his work of redemption. First, we see the Incarnation as a demonstration of God's desire to identify with and redeem his creation (John 1:14). More specifically, God desires to redeem a people for himself (John 10:16). The work of redemption includes the Father "transferr[ing] us into the kingdom of the Son" in whom "we have redemption, the forgiveness of sins" (Col. 1:13–14). This work also includes the Spirit's regeneration and work of opening our eyes to the beauty and love of God because he has been poured forth into our hearts (Rom. 5:5). This means as well that God is knitting us into a new community with new relationships and responsibilities to one another. Hence, we are called brothers and sisters in Christ (Rom. 8:28; Heb. 2:11). Collectively, we have a new mission in this world: to glorify God by proclaiming the hope of the gospel in the power of the Spirit. This leads us to consider how confessing God as Trinity impacts our practice of formation.

Trinity and Formation

All Christians, from the pew to the pulpit, need to have a basic yet firm grasp on God as triune if we want to be serious about spiritual formation. A disciple can love the Lord her God with all her heart, soul, mind, and strength and not be versed on the finer points of Trinitarian theology. But if God has revealed himself as Father, Son, and Spirit, then it demands that we be as faithful as possible to understand what that means for our lives. I love what theologian Bruce Demarest has to say about how the Trinity relates to our Christian life: "Through the grace of the new birth, followers of Jesus are swept into the loving relational life of the Trinity and so participate in this radically transforming culture of grace."[9] I want to be a part of a "radically transforming culture of grace" and I want others to be a part as well. This is what it means to hold fast to the triune God and participate in his life and see his truth, beauty, and goodness infiltrate and shape our lives. The triune God has invited us by his goodness into the story of redemption, which is the story of our formation. Let's look now at two practical ways the Trinity informs our Christian formation: our life of community and our life of mission.

---

9. Bruce Demarest, "The Trinity as Foundation for Spiritual Formation" in *The Kingdom Life: A Practical Theology of Discipleship and Spiritual Formation*, ed. Alan Andrews (Colorado Springs, CO: NavPress, 2016), 250.

Trinity and Community

The Trinity provides a blueprint and gives shape to our life of community in the church. I will have some additional considerations for community and formation in chapter 5. For now, we must grasp the basic idea that we have a communal identity wrapped up in the work of the triune God. Paul describes this identity in Ephesians: "There is one body and one Spirit—just as you were called to one hope at your calling—one Lord, one faith, one baptism, one God and Father of all, who is above all and through all and in all" (4:4–6). Our basic Christian life and experience is based on the triune God, his inner life and external work in the world. Our fellowship as brothers and sisters is intended to mirror the fellowship of the Godhead, united with the goal of glorifying God. Because there is one body and one Spirit, we should work

> "Because God has already laid the foundation of our fellowship, because God has bound us together in one body with other Christians in Jesus Christ, long before we entered into common life with them, we enter into that common life not as demanders but as thankful recipients."
> —Dietrich Bonhoeffe[10]

---

10. Dietrich Bonhoeffer, *Life Together: The Classic Exploration of Christian Community* (New York: Harper One, 1954), 28.

toward unity and be wary of disunity and dysfunction. Because there is one hope and one faith, we should be diligent about teaching sound Christian doctrine and forming believers to hold to true gospel hope. Because there is one Lord and one baptism, we should be diligent to practice unity around the core gospel message with other believers.

The mark of our fellowship in the community of faith, baptism, is itself a Trinitarian declaration. Jesus commanded his church to make disciples, "baptizing them in the name of the Father and of the Son and of the Holy Spirit" (Matt. 28:19).[11] From the moment of conversion, we are initiated into the life of the Trinity. As we regularly recall our baptism, we are reminded that we exist in the name and life of the Father, Son, and Holy Spirit. Having received baptism and committed to a life of following Christ, we are now welcome to the table of the Lord where we continually remember his substitutionary death until he returns. Our practice of Communion is based on our salvation in Christ and points us back to the redemptive work of the Trinity. It is the place where the Spirit further reminds us of and applies to us the work of Christ, prompting us toward further Christlikeness. I will discuss the role of Communion in spiritual formation more in chapter 5, but I will always be an advocate for weekly Communion in the gathered worship of the church. We can never have too many reminders and opportunities to reflect on the work of redemption. The Lord's Supper is a family practice, something that welds the community of faith ever tighter, and is a communal

---

11. For more on this idea, see Scott R. Swain, *The Trinity: An Introduction* (Wheaton, IL: Crossway, 2020), 28–34.

reminder of our life together in God through Christ. Give me a church that takes the regular practice of the Lord's Supper seriously, with all its profound theological and practical facets, and I will show you a community that is thriving and effective in its formation of Christ-followers.

A final, and often neglected, way that the Trinity impacts our formation in community is our hospitality. Our hospitality and greeting one another is based on the triune God welcoming us into his family, having been adopted "through Jesus Christ for himself, according to the good pleasure of his will, to the praise of his glorious grace that he lavished on us in the Beloved One" (Eph. 1:5–6). Paul says to "welcome one another, just as Christ also welcomed you, to the glory of God"

> The mark of our fellowship in the community of faith, baptism, is itself a Trinitarian declaration.

(Rom. 15:7). The writer of Hebrews exhorts the church: "Don't neglect to show hospitality, for by doing this some have welcomed angels as guests without knowing it" (Heb. 13:2). The work of redemption is itself an act of cosmic hospitality. Because we have been ushered into the family of God by his grace and mercy, we are called to extend the same grace and mercy to others. This begins by greeting and welcoming others into the fellowship, whether it be the first time or the hundredth. Too often we give the ministry of hospitality and greeting to anyone with a pulse. I'm all for people growing into service roles within the church, but a ministry of hospitality is too important to assign to the nearest warm body. When we don't equip people in the church to be hospitable and understand the significance of welcoming others, we fail to present the welcoming nature of the triune God. The gospel often begins with a handshake. The most theological thing one can do is to cultivate a significant and meaningful ministry of hospitality in the church. Rosaria Butterfield, in her book *The Gospel Comes with a House Key*, drives this hospitality point home: "Radically ordinary hospitality shows this skeptical, post-Christian world what authentic Christianity looks like."[12] All throughout the New Testament, the church and its leaders are called to demonstrate hospitality. Hospitality is more than a cultural curiosity, it is a gospel priority.

> Because we have been ushered into the family of God by his grace and mercy, we are called to extend the same grace and mercy to others.

Six priorities emerge from these three general ways the Trinity impacts our community life. The first priority is *unity*. Because there is a unity of persons in the Godhead, all members of Christ's body should strive for unity in the same biblical vision and goals for God's mission in the world and care for one another (see Eph. 4:1–3). The second priority is

---

12. Rosaria Butterfield, *The Gospel Comes with a House Key: Practicing Radically Ordinary Hospitality in Our Post-Christian World* (Wheaton, IL: Crossway, 2018), 13.

diversity. Because every person of the Godhead has a distinct role, all members of Christ's body should understand that diversity within the church is to be cherished and encouraged (see Rom. 12:3–8). The third priority for our community life is *equality*. Since every member of the Godhead is equal in glory and honor, all members of Christ's body should seek to honor one another as image-bearers with unique and valuable gifts (see Gal. 3:28). The fourth priority has to do with *ability*. Because of the work of God through the Spirit in giving gifts to the church, all members of Christ's body must recognize, honor, and promote the range of abilities and gifts present within the body (see 1 Cor. 12:12–31). The fifth priority is *humility*. Because the Son displayed the ultimate act of humility in the Incarnation, all members of Christ's body should seek to serve the good of one another and not count themselves greater than anyone else (see Phil. 2:1–4). The sixth and final priority is *mobility*. Because the Father sent the Son and the Father and Son sent the Spirit, all members of Christ's body must be willing to understand the mission of God as a call to go and tell others of God's glorious story of redemption (Matt. 28:19–20). This final priority point leads me to consider another important facet of our formation based on the Trinity: our mission.

Trinity and Mission

Knowing God as Trinity also impacts our understanding of Christian mission. Biblical scholar Christopher Wright states: "We humans have a mission on earth because God had a purpose in putting us on it."[13] Because we bear the image of God, we have a mission and mandate to make him known and display his beauty in the world. What theologians have called the "economic Trinity" is how we view the mission of God in the world. By using the word *economic*, we're not talking about how God helps us with IRA plans and stock options, but how the economy or work of God is shown in the plan of redemption. Theologian Scott Swain puts it this way: "The works of God are not a matter of three friends getting together, each doing his part, to accomplish a common goal. Nor are the works of God the exhibition of an indistinct force. The works of God are the works of the thrice-holy Trinity."[14] This relates to what theologians call the "appropriations" of God, meaning that God appropriates certain roles to highlight the Persons of the Godhead. Swain notes: "Certain works of the Trinity are associated with certain persons of the Trinity because those works specially manifest the personal properties of the specific persons."[15] The Father is the sender; the Son, the one who is sent; and the Spirit, the sanctifier. These actions show the unique qualities of each Person yet also demonstrate their united purpose. God is a sending God. God also sends his people into the world to bear witness to his sending of Christ for our redemption. Thus, our spiritual formation should always lean in the direction of going and telling.

---

13. Christopher J. H. Wright, *The Mission of God's People: A Biblical Theology of the Church's Mission* (Grand Rapids, MI: Zondervan Academic, 2010), 50.

14. Swain, *The Trinity*, 108.

15. Swain, 112.

Mission is primarily God's action, and this divine action forms the identity of the church. Jesus gives the church its Great Commission: "Go, therefore, and make disciples of all nations, baptizing them in the name of the Father and of the Son and of the Holy Spirit, teaching them to observe everything I have commanded you. And remember, I am with you always, to the end of the age" (Matt. 28:19–20). As previously mentioned, this commission includes the Trinitarian mark of baptism for all who become disciples of Christ. So we see how this mission is undergirded by the triune God, and it becomes our enduring assignment until Christ returns. While the Great Commission is a firm rallying cry for world missions, as it should be, I think it's even better to see it as the all-encompassing mission of formation for Christ's disciples.

Mission is connected to the gospel story, a story that is for the entire world. Thus, it takes a worldwide church to share the gospel story and meet the needs of others through mission. As Wright notes: "The mission of God in the world is vast. So he has called and commissioned a people—originally the descendants of Abraham, now a multinational global community in Christ. And it is through the *whole* of those people that God is working his mission purposes out, in all their diversity. Of course every individual cannot do everything."[16] The mission is vast, but this is why the church has been empowered by the Spirit of the living God. And lest you think this means you must "go big or go home" in your missional participation, it

---

16. Christopher J. H. Wright, *The Mission of God: Unlocking the Bible's Grand Narrative* (Downers Grove, IL: IVP Academic, 2013), 322; emphasis in original.

will take people going across the street just as much as people going across the world to accomplish God's gospel mission. All are sent, yet some are sent by staying. The history of missions is filled with those who both left home as well as stayed home to share the gospel with the lost. The mission of God must include people who travel to faraway lands to put down roots for a church plant as well as those who travel to Walmart to pick up root beer for a block party, all for the sake of reaching people with the gospel. The mission of the triune God calls for both, and everything in between. If the church understands its identity as bound up in the Trinity, that identity will spill over into missional activity.

Trinitarian Training

The late nineteenth-century Dutch theologian Herman Bavinck said, "Now in the confession of the Trinity we hear the heartbeat of the Christian religion: every error results from, or upon deeper reflection is traceable to, a departure in the doctrine of the Trinity."[17] To maintain "the faith that was delivered to the saints once for all" (Jude 3) is a serious matter. While the doctrine of the Trinity directly relates to our understanding of God and salvation, it also has significant implications for our life. We have briefly noted how it impacts our view of community and mission in the church. These are two significant areas of spiritual formation. We will discuss

---

17. Herman Bavinck, *Reformed Dogmatics*, vol. 2, God and Creation, eds. John Bolt and John Vriend (Grand Rapids, MI: Baker Academic, 2004), 288.

related doctrines of union with Christ and sanctification and their role in Christian spiritual formation in the next chapters. That said, I want to give one final encouragement as we consider the need for imprinting Trinitarian doctrine in our hearts and minds. We must consistently and unapologetically teach, preach, sing, pray to and talk about God as Triune. If you are a ministry leader, take regular opportunities to teach basic Trinitarian doctrine. If you are a preacher, consider preaching a regular sermon on the Trinity and taking every opportunity to highlight Trinitarian connections in your sermons. And all Christians should regularly study the Scripture to see the triune God more clearly, as well as read good books on the Trinity along the way.

J. T. English says, "The next curriculum, the next conference, or the next community group will only help you grow deeper in your relationship with Christ insofar as it attempts to reorient your love toward the triune God."[18] While every teaching doesn't have to focus on Trinitarian doctrine, all our ministry and training efforts should be directed toward helping others love the God who is Father, Son, and Spirit. If you have the resources and space, teach classes (or entire training programs) that emphasize the foundational truth of the Trinity for Christian life and practice. Ask worship leaders to sing hymns and songs that are serious about Trinitarian doctrine. Especially if you are the one tasked with leading worship, your influence upon the way people know God is immense. I agree with Reeves's assertion: "[The] triune nature of this God

18. J. T. English, *Deep Discipleship: How the Church Can Make Whole Disciples of Jesus* (Nashville, TN: B&H Books, 2020), 20.

affects everything from how we listen to music to how we pray: it makes for happier marriages, warmer dealings with others, better church life; it gives Christians assurance, shapes holiness and transforms the very way we look at the world around us."[19] I firmly believe that we can't have too much Trinitarian teaching and formation in the church, but we can certainly have too little. Teaching on the Trinity does not come at the expense of Bible study, evangelism training, or missions. In fact, good Trinitarian formation will lead you to richer study of Scripture, more fervent gospel witness, and more consistent and faithful missional engagement. It is always the case that a better understanding and love for God leads to a better understanding and love for his Word and love for others. When we deprive people of the mystery and wonder of the triune God, we deprive them of a spiritually vibrant life.

> When we deprive people of the mystery and wonder of the triune God, we deprive them of a spiritually vibrant life.

Final Thoughts

The doctrine of the Trinity *is* the Christian doctrine of God. Matthew Barrett notes: "As long as we bear the label *evangelical*, we also believe in a gospel that is trinitarian

---

19. Reeves, *Delighting in the Trinity*, 10.

through and through."[20] It hurts the church when we rob them of the mystery of God. Ice cube and clover leaf illustrations aside, we should be serious about Christian spiritual formation centered upon the profound glory of the triune God. The doctrine of the Trinity matters for our Christian life in myriad ways. Tragically, we have not done justice to the doctrine of the Trinity and the effects have shown. Theologian Fred Sanders notes how the Trinity and Trinitarian doctrine are often absent from evangelical church life. He observes: "To many evangelicals, the stakes of thinking about the Trinity seem too high and the payoff too low . . . No wonder many of our congregations drift from year to year with only the vaguest apprehension of the fact that their Christian life is one of communion with the Father in the Son and Spirit."[21] From giving shape to our community, to our mission, to the ongoing ministry of the church, if we lose focus on the Trinity, it will be to our peril. The Trinity *is* a big deal! The mission that the triune God has given us is also a big deal. For spiritual formation to be Christian, it must at all turns keep its attention on the triune God. As we move forward in understanding doctrinal foundations for Christian formation, we will see how our union with Christ and the work of the Spirit are subsequent doctrines that flow from understanding God as Trinity.

---

20. Matthew Barrett, *Simply Trinity: The Unmanipulated Father, Son, and Spirit* (Grand Rapids, MI: Baker Books, 2021), 104.

21. Fred Sanders, *The Deep Things of God: How the Trinity Changes Everything*, 2nd ed. (Wheaton, IL: Crossway, 2017), 14.

Resources for Further Study

Matthew Barrett. *Simply Trinity: The Unmanipulated Father, Son, and Spirit*. Grand Rapids, MI: Baker Books, 2021.

Michael Reeves. *Delighting in the Trinity: An Introduction to the Christian Faith*. Downers Grove, IL: IVP Academic, 2012.

Fred Sanders. *The Deep Things of God: How the Trinity Changes Everything*. 2nd ed. Wheaton, IL: Crossway, 2017.

Peter Sanlon. *Simply God: Recovering the Classical Trinity*. Nottingham, UK: InterVarsity Press, 2014.

Scott R. Swain. *The Trinity: An Introduction*. Wheaton, IL: Crossway, 2020.

Questions for Reflection

1. According to this chapter, what makes the Trinity foundational for understanding spiritual formation?

2. What has been your experience learning about the Trinity in your local church? What sermons/classes/songs/etc. stand out to you?

3. How might knowing God as Trinity help you in your understanding of salvation? Of formation and discipleship?

4. What makes the Trinity a compelling foundation for community in the local church? Which postures or marks of Trinitarian community are difficult for you?

5. How might a Trinitarian understanding of Christian mission help you better grasp the connection between mission and spiritual formation?

CHAPTER 3

Getting Union with Christ Right for Formation

Without knowledge of self there is no knowledge of God.
Without knowledge of God there is no knowledge of self.
—JOHN CALVIN[1]

Union with Christ is at the heart of the biblical doctrine
of salvation.
—ROBERT LETHAM[2]

Our age is grasping for identity. The word *identity* itself is present in much of our political and cultural conversations. From identity politics to gender identity to even identity fraud, we are very concerned about our identity. Movies and TV shows explore the theme of identity, whether it's El

---

1. John Calvin, *Institutes of the Christian Religion*, 1.1.1.
2. Robert Letham, *Systematic Theology* (Wheaton, IL: Crossway, 2019).

59

from *Stranger Things* or Elsa from *Frozen*. From talk shows to tabloids, we are all seeking ultimate meaning for our life. Let's take, for example, the conversation of gender identity in our culture today. Not that long ago, the sort of conversations that are normal would have been unthinkable. We can not only choose our own gender identity, but we can also decide if we want to have a gender at all. You may shake your head and dismiss gender ideology as trendy or faddish, but it reveals another facet of the persistent question of identity in our culture. Philosopher Charles Taylor has called our age a "secular age," where there is a rejection of a cosmological meta-narrative guiding our thoughts and actions in the world.[3] What Taylor and others have observed is that our culture has lost a sense of otherworldliness and mystery. There are no forces (let alone a transcendent God) guiding our lives and circumstances. We are in this for ourselves by ourselves. Rather than freeing humanity, this "secular" view of the world has created a crushing burden and has led us deeper into the crisis of identity.

Christians should not be surprised that people struggle with identity. The question of identity is as old as time, as Satan tempted Eve to question who she was and the mandate given to her and Adam as image-bearers of God. "Did God really say . . . ?" (Gen. 3:1) is the demonic whisper that permeates all questions of identity. Many of our problems are rooted in mistaken identity. Apart from an intimate relationship

---

3. For a summary of Charles Taylor and his work on secularism, see James K. A. Smith, *How (Not) to be Secular: Reading Charles Taylor* (Grand Rapids, MI: Wm. B. Eerdmans, 2014).

with God through Christ, the tension of false identity will never be resolved. In fact, this is the crux of the gospel message. Christians should understand most of all that identity is found in Christ alone. By trusting in the person and work of Jesus Christ, placing our allegiance in him as Lord, we gain a new identity in the world with a renewed sense of purpose in it. The Spirit continually applies the work of Christ and drills the eternal truth of our union with Christ deeper into our hearts. Before we look at the doctrine of union with Christ and its implications, let us take a step back and look at an even more foundational doctrine for understanding the dilemma of identity in our world today.

Image-Bearers

In Genesis 1:26 God said, "Let us make man in our image, according to our likeness." This design, the *imago dei* or image of God, is intrinsic to who we are as humans. Our basic identity is bound up in the creative genius of the triune God. The account of Creation in Genesis also describes mankind as containing the breath of God (2:7). We are theomorphic creatures—formed by God and containing his breath. Because of this, humanity is distinct from all other creatures and is alone capable of a deep relationship with one another and with God. Because of the *imago dei*, every person has value. As male and female, God gave mankind a mandate to create and cultivate. We represent God and have been given a mission by God as his representatives. We get to do *God-like* things with *God-made* stuff. We till the soil of God's original creation to develop, grow, and create new and exciting things. From Tesla plants to turnip patches, humanity imitates God in our creative work. In the Creation account, humanity is the pinnacle of God's creative work, given abilities that no other creature possesses. The *imago dei* grounds our basic identity and our knowledge of self. It also means we have the potential for virtue and growth, acting in ways in accordance with God's will. The creation of humanity as image-bearers of God grants us permission to pursue what is good, true, and beautiful. We have value, vocation, and the potential for virtue because of God's design.

It was because of our divinely gifted abilities that humanity took that fateful step away from God in rebellion. The Fall created a fracture in the very fabric of the cosmos. Because of sin, we are alienated from God, from creation, and from one another. In God's grace and mercy, he continued to sustain and provide for his creation and promised a Redeemer who would restore all things and establish the peace and justice of God once again on earth (see Gen. 3:15; 1 Pet. 1:18–20; Rev. 22:1–5).

> We till the soil of God's original creation to develop, grow, and create new and exciting things.

The aching question of identity in our culture is rooted in the Fall. Because "all have sinned and fall short of the glory of God" (Rom. 3:23), everything, from our hearts and minds to our bodies to our relationships, has been radically affected by sin. We have become fractured and have lost the unity we had with God. There is not one area of our life and experience left untouched by sin. Because of sin, we have a heart that is disordered and bent toward itself. We love the wrong things. We seek after false beauty. We find hope in things that are ultimately hopeless. We retain the same basic concepts, have basic abilities to do good things and think rationally, but our hearts are turned in on themselves. Even the best of our actions is tainted with sin, selfishness, and pride. The reason we are still able to do anything good and have societies that function at some level is because we are made in the image of God and retain this basic design and divine imprint. But apart from a restorative work of grace in our lives, we will always be at the mercy of false ideologies, vain philosophies, and cultural dogmas that can never provide us a true and meaningful identity. Only in union with Christ will our identity be restored. When we are united with Christ by grace through faith (see Eph. 2:8), we can once again live for what we were made for: peace and unity with God and one another.

Union with Christ: The Heart of the Gospel

In his book *Union with Christ: The Way to Know and Enjoy God*, author Rankin Wilbourne describes his rediscovery of the doctrine of union with Christ. He confesses: "I was much more accustomed to thinking of Christ as a savior *outside* of me than as one who dwells *within* and has united his life to mine."[4] Upon discovering older authors such as John Calvin

---

4. Rankin Wilbourne, *Union with Christ: The Way to Know and Enjoy God* (Colorado Springs, CO: David C. Cook, 2016), Kindle loc. 346; emphasis in original.

and Jonathan Edwards and their constant refrain of union with Christ, Wilbourne came to understand that the doctrine of union with Christ "is not some dusty relic of history or ivory tower pursuit" but rather "takes us to the very heart of the gospel."[5] Perhaps you are just like Wilbourne, having grown up thinking of Christ as remotely exterior rather than intimately interior. Perhaps we've prioritized the message of "accepting Jesus into our hearts" at the expense of "accepting Jesus as dwelling in our hearts." The doctrine of union with Christ is the most profound yet practical of Christian truths. It states that God has united us to himself in Christ and that we now have all the benefits, treasures, and privileges of being a son or daughter of God. "The greatest treasure of the gospel, greater than any other benefit the gospel brings," according to Wilbourne, "is the gift of God himself."[6]

Union has everything to do with identity. The doctrine of union with Christ tells us that identity is based on God's work and not ours. Though we might have things that distinguish us from other people (including biological sex, language, and ethnicity), these things are subservient to our ultimate identity in Christ. This is Paul's encouragement to the Galatian church to help them understand the implications of their union with Christ: "For those of you who were baptized into Christ have been clothed with Christ. There is no Jew or Greek, slave or free, male and female; since you are all one in Christ Jesus" (Gal. 3:27–28). Paul is not eradicating the realities of what it means to be a man or a woman, nor is he erasing cultural

---

5. Wilbourne, Kindle loc. 365.
6. Wilbourne, Kindle loc. 372.

differences among Jewish or Greek peoples, nor is he being thoughtless as to the realities of slavery in a Greco-Roman society. The issue is that we are prone to make each of these things a standard of our identity. The only identity that matters most, the one that defines who we are, the one that is most true and meaningful, is our identity in Christ. Paul personalizes this when he states: "I have been crucified with Christ, and I no longer live, but Christ lives in me. The life I now live in the body, I live by faith in the Son of God, who loved me and gave himself for me" (Gal. 2:20).

As we look at the New Testament, we see five basic ways that union with Christ is understood:

1. Union is the primary understanding of our salvation (Rom. 5–8; Eph. 2:1–10)
2. Union is the basis of our identity (Eph. 4:20–24; Col. 1:13; 1 Pet. 1:3–5)
3. Union is the grounds of the ongoing work of Christ in our lives (Col. 3:1–17)
4. Union is the foundation of our peace, comfort, and assurance (Phil. 4:7; Eph. 2:11–22, 4:1–6)
5. Union is the cornerstone of Christian discipleship and formation (Eph. 2:19–22, 4:15; Col. 1:9–23)

Gregg Allison summarizes the doctrine of union with Christ and its benefits: "Through union, believers are identified with Christ's death, burial, resurrection, and ascension, and God communicates all his blessings of salvation . . . Christ dwells in those whom he is united, and then in turn dwell in him."[7] Union with Christ is a work of grace through and through. Union communicates what is true about us now and for eternity. Union with Christ is the proof of God's goodness toward his people and tells us that God is with us no matter what.

So, what makes identity with Christ so fundamental to Christian spiritual formation? There is no way we can pursue Christian spiritual formation apart from grasping our union with Christ. Formation that focuses on decisions for Christ at the expense of union with Christ will leave people wandering in a desert away from Christ. The oasis of the Christian life is union with Jesus. It brings joy, assurance, and fruitfulness. A decision to follow Christ is essential, but that decision leads to the awareness of Christ's work in us. For Christian formation to take root, we must emphasize, at every angle of church ministry, the profound nature of our identity in Christ and our perpetual union with him. Before we explore some pitfalls and cautions, I want to further explain why grasping our union is so pivotal for spiritual formation.

Union and Discipleship

In the late 1980s and 1990s, the "WWJD" bracelet made its way on the scene of the Christian subculture. The question of "What Would Jesus Do?" was intended to encourage

---

7. Gregg Allison, "Union with Christ" in *The Baker Compact Dictionary of Theological Terms* (Grand Rapids, MI: Baker Books, 2016), 215–16.

Christians to live out an ethic that looked and acted like Jesus. The notion of imitating Christ in Christian spirituality is as old as the New Testament. There is, of course, nothing wrong with wanting to imitate our Savior in his thoughts and actions. I sported a few WWJDs in the '90s myself, and I continue to see them worn to this day. I never doubt the sincerity of those who wear the band, and in many ways, it shows their desire to honor the Lord with their lives. In my experience, however, the "WWJD" ethic has the tendency to make spiritual formation more about external actions apart from internal transformation. While bracelets and jewelry can remind one of their faith, that faith has to be internalized first. Internal transformation must precede external imitation. We need union with Christ before we need a bracelet about him.

We have a new identity based on our union with Christ. And because we have a new identity through our union, we now belong to a new family. Paul declares: "He predestined us to be adopted as sons through Jesus Christ for himself, according to the good pleasure of his will" (Eph. 1:5). We've been adopted into a new family—the greatest family—and with this new family comes a new set of family values and family practices. Think about your own family and their habits. Almost all of us have some sort of ritual around the Thanksgiving and Christmas holidays. Maybe we travel to a certain family member's house every year, have a certain holiday movie we watch, and expect to eat a lot of coma-inducing food and watch a lot of football. Our family habits and rituals show others what we value.

While watching *Elf* and the Dallas Cowboys on Thanksgiving is good to do, the family of God practices habits and rituals that contribute more to our eternal happiness than pumpkin pie ever could. Union with Christ means we now exist eternally in the family of God—a new and lasting identity. Because we have a new identity and new values, we have a new vision for living in the world. Now that we have a new vision for living, we are freed to see other stories and "visions" for what they are: false and desolate. Our union transforms our hearts to see the beauty and grace of God "because the law of the Spirit of life in Christ Jesus has set you free from the law of sin and death" (Rom. 8:2). Since Christians have new family values, we have new habits and rituals that coincide with those values. This is the life of Christian spiritual formation, living out the values of the family of God through the habits and rituals given to us by God. Union necessitates an active spirituality based on an objective reality. We will get into this more in chapters 5 and 6.

Our culture today, however, presents us with one major roadblock to avoid when it comes to how we understand union and spiritual formation. I believe we will never exhaust the riches of our union in our preaching, teaching, counseling, and discipleship ministries. There are ways, however, that we can confuse our union with cultural notions of "authenticity." Let's turn to consider this significant roadblock and how it can arrest our formation in Christ based on our union with Christ.

A Spiritual Roadblock:
A Culture of Authenticity

When I began vocational ministry, I felt like I heard and saw the word *authentic* at every ministry conference and in every popular ministry book I read. Ministry success was based on being an authentic individual, creating authentic ministry spaces, and preaching and teaching in an authentic way. The word *authentic* in these spaces was usually defined as "not holding back" or "being real" or "allowing space to be one-self." So, what's so bad about being authentic? Isn't this a value that we should cherish? Isn't the opposite of being authentic being fake and false? While I'm not against the idea of being authentic as opposed to being false, the idea of authenticity can take on a life that can go against biblical values. The major problem is that we live in a culture today that has redefined what it means to be authentic in a subjective and self-fulfilling manner. And in this redefined paradigm of authenticity, the effects to our spiritual formation can be damaging and long-lasting. Let me explain.

I'm sure it's no surprise to you when I say that we live in a highly self-indulgent culture. None of us is immune. Not only do we expect our online orders to arrive the same day, but we also expect people to agree with everything we say lest they be "canceled" or muted. We also expect government and financial institutions, with minimal efforts on our part, to guarantee and create systems which maximize our pleasure and minimize our pain. Though we might say that "pain is gain" or that "whatever doesn't kill you makes you stronger," in essence, none of us really wants that to be true. We are seeking all the ways we can to bring fulfillment to our lives without the experience of discomfort. Hence, we need to be true to ourselves and remove every barrier that inhibits our happiness and our personalized stories of the Good Life. If we do not have what we want or are not the kind of person we want to be, we should be free—indeed, *guaranteed* the right—to do what we want and be whoever we wish to be.

Philosopher Charles Taylor, in his book *The Ethics of Authenticity*, discusses how the notion of authenticity has devolved in our culture. He observes where we are today: "Being true to myself means being true to my own originality, and that is something only I can articulate and discover. In articulating it, I am also defining myself. I am realizing a potentiality that is properly my own. This is the background understanding to the modern ideal of authenticity, and to the goals of self-fulfilment [*sic*] or self-realization in which it is usually couched."[8] Charles Taylor, writing in the early 1990s, observed then what has become pervasive today: unless one is true to how they feel and view themselves, then they are inauthentic. This has become the rallying cry of the transgender movement in modern times.[9] It's also the basic ethic that undergirds most music, film, and popular culture today. Our culture is obsessed with the notion of authenticity. Because radical autonomy and freedom of choice are inherent within our experience, we need to be free to express our "true self." At

---

8. Charles Taylor, *The Ethics of Authenticity* (Cambridge, MA: Harvard University Press, 1991), 29.

9. For more on this, see Carl Trueman, *Strange New World: How Thinkers and Activists Redefined Identity and Sparked the Sexual Revolution* (Wheaton, IL: Crossway, 2022).

the expense of all else, we should have the unquestioned right to be self-actualized. And lest we fool ourselves, this notion of authenticity has infiltrated the church in various ways. There are four issues with our current culture of authenticity that can impact the church and stunt our spiritual formation.

The first issue is that there is no true gauge for how to be "authentic." There will always be someone who is more authentic than you in this kind of culture. No one can objectively determine authenticity in this environment, and the multiplicity of choices and identity options creates more burdens than freedoms.[10] The norms of authenticity are ever-changing, and the only way to keep up is to forfeit your sanity. Evidence of ever-changing norms can be found on magazine covers and among "influencer" social media accounts. It feels like every issue or post promises a way to be the best you, only to offer different tips the next month. There is no way one can keep track of all the ways to be the best version of yourself and remain stable. Diet strategies, fashion guides, dating advice, best vacations, and more promise to only give a shadow of what union with Christ can deliver: peace and stability.

The second issue is related: a culture of authenticity easily slides into narcissism and elitism. In the science-fiction television show, *Black Mirror*, the creators take current-day ideas and play them out a few years in the future to see what could be. In the episode entitled "Nosedive," the worth and

---

10. While not specifically dealing with the culture of authenticity and identity, the idea of how unlimited choices actually harms us is explored at length in Barry Shultz, *The Paradox of Choice: Why More Is Less* (New York, NY: HarperCollins, 2004).

status of a person is based on their social media rating. One's job, housing, and even quality of travel is determined upon social media likes. A young professional named Lacie seeks to climb the social ladder by impressing an old high school friend who is at the top of this social rating system. Initially all goes well until a series of unfortunate circumstances cause people around Lacie to give her low social ratings, which then causes her to "nosedive" into social no-man's-land, ultimately landing her in jail. The episode, though fictional, rings true to our culture in many ways. Those who are perceived as more authentic become the elites of society, with others desperately seeking their approval or trying to live up to their standards.

It also generates a culture of extreme narcissism. Narcissism is the nuclear power source of social media. It's no wonder that the culture of authenticity now coincides with the rise of entertainment, technology, and social media. While smartphones and social media bring positive benefits, they can also lead to a false sense of authenticity, bending toward narcissism. Tony Reinke, in his *12 Ways Your Phone Is Changing You*, notes the allure of self-approval which can feed narcissism. He observes: "Smartphones prick the primitive human impulse for appreciation—self-replication in order to be seen, known, and loved—through constant contact with other seekers of affirmation."[11] We want people to love us, which is not a bad thing, but this need devolves into a constant impulse, which further devolves into a complete fascination with ourselves and the way others perceive us. Only in union with

---

11. Tony Reinke, *12 Ways Your Phone Is Changing You* (Wheaton, IL: Crossway, 2017), 77.

Christ can we be truly known and be loved in the right ways by the right Person.

The third issue with authenticity relates to God's sovereignty. In a modern culture of authenticity, we can easily reject God's sovereignty in terms of biological gender, family experience, trials, and seasons of suffering. The current spirit of authenticity sees all such "norms" and circumstances as potential shackles to break and barriers to overcome. Your biological sex is a hindrance to who you want to be. The suffering you experience is something to be transcended. Friends, family, even spouses and children are tangential to your happiness and expression of authenticity. Whatever inhibits you from self-actualization and fulfillment should be dismissed, divorced, or discarded. So much damage is done in the wake of living an "authentic" life in this fashion, and its effects can be felt in the church. "I am no longer satisfied in this marriage." "This church is not meeting my needs anymore." "If God wants me to be happy, he wouldn't allow this suffering in my life." I have heard these exact phrases, or variations of them, throughout my pastoral ministry. Certainly, there may be deep spiritual issues that underlie these sentiments, and I would not casually dismiss them. Our culture of authenticity feeds these sorts of responses. When we dismiss how God uses the circumstances of our life within his sovereign plan, we

> **Only in union with Christ can we be truly known and be loved in the right ways by the right Person.**

circumvent his goodness and providence. When we understand the beauty and profundity of our union with Christ, we
come to rest in the promise that "all things work together for
the good of those who love God, who are called according to
his purpose" (Rom. 8:28).

The final issue with authenticity is the denial of biblical anthropology. Rather than being created male and female
in God's image as the Bible teaches (Gen. 1:27), authenticity in today's world rejects the body in favor of some inner
feeling or spiritual insight. This idea of authenticity is most
directly connected to the religious belief of Gnosticism, an
ancient belief that humans are nothing more than spiritual
creatures imprisoned by flesh. The word *gnosis* comes from the
Greek word for knowledge and, hence, focuses on salvation
through special knowledge. Gnosticism impacted Jewish and
Christian thought in various ways, and so-called "Christian"
Gnostics sought to imprint their false teaching with Christian
vocabulary. Therefore, Jesus was the one who came to save
mankind through special knowledge, not through his atonement on the cross and bodily resurrection from the grave.
In fact, in most gnostic teaching, Jesus was just one of many
spiritual beings. There is much more to the history and teaching of Gnosticism, but its effects can still be felt today. In
today's culture of authenticity, our body, our experience, and
other material realities do not matter as much as what we feel
on the inside. To be truly authentic is to discover one's inner
reality, and either alter our body to conform or deny that our
body or material existence matter. There are many ways the
gnostic tendency has infiltrated the church and its ministry,

and we don't have space to explore all those issues, but we see Gnosticism play out whenever we prioritize inner spirituality to the neglect of the body.

Having explored the spiritual roadblock of authenticity (at least as our culture perceives it), I want to offer two encouragements as to how our union impacts our formation. In sum, our union with Christ makes our formation not only possible, but it also makes it rich and meaningful and touches every aspect of our lives and ministry.

Our True Self in Christ

Being authentic is not bad insofar as we are defining it in relation to our union with Christ. If we take authenticity on the culture's terms, we will find ourselves in murky waters. If we understand, however, that Christ in us *is* the best version of ourselves, then we will be free to live in God's goodness for us. The redemptive story of God and union with Christ is the only secure answer to a modern culture of authenticity. Christian psychologist David Benner reflects on the idea of authenticity in his book *The Gift of Being Yourself.* Benner asserts that our "true" or "authentic" self is the self that is in Christ. Benner says, "Our true self-in-Christ is the only self that will support authenticity. It alone provides an identity that is eternal."[12] Our union with Christ does not turn us into Jesus robots but, rather, frees us to be who God made us in Christ. Each of us is "remarkably and wondrously made" (Ps. 139:14) in God's image, with unique gifts and abilities. In Christ, our

---

12. David G. Benner, *The Gift of Being Yourself: The Sacred Call to Self-Discovery*, expanded ed. (Downers Grove: IVP Books, 2015), 17.

personality is not erased but enhanced. In Christ, our gifts are not jettisoned but harnessed. In Christ, our desires are not suppressed but redirected. Truly, our union with Christ seeks to conform us to the image of Christ (Rom. 8:29), but that process does not obliterate us—it completes us. In Christ, we are made into the humans we were always intended to be with Christ as the blueprint. This is the difference between the old self and new self, which is "being renewed in knowledge according to the image of your Creator" (Col. 3:10). As Benner observes: "[As] we become more like Christ we become more uniquely our own true self."[13]

While this is true, we all run into the "Romans 7" problem. As Paul explains in Romans 7, we functionally exist in two realms. Though God has rescued and redeemed us, we still wrestle against the flesh. We are all children of Adam, and though the new Adam has come, the ghost of the first Adam remains. Paul observes that there is a war waging within us, even though inside we delight (and are growing in our delight of) God's law (vv. 22–23). The waging war will not last forever, as we have hope in the final redemption of our bodies and the expectation of dwelling with God forever in a new heaven and new earth (see Rom. 8:23; 2 Pet. 3:13). Therefore, as we grow in our delight of God and wage war against sin, we can rest assured that the Spirit is working through us based on our union with Christ (see Rom. 5:1–11). We will discuss the role of the Spirit and sanctification in the next chapter, but our union with Christ ensures that our growth in holiness

---

13. Benner, *The Gift of Being Yourself*, 17.

is taking place. That leads us to briefly discuss the practical implications of our formation based on our union with Christ.

Our True Formation in Christ

Biblical scholar David Peterson notes: "Practical holiness means working out in everyday life and relationships the moral consequences of our union with Christ."[14] Through our union, we have "received the Spirit of adoption" (Rom 8:15), which casts out fear, doubt, and shame. This may not be automatic or immediate, but it is a foundation of our union with Christ. Hence, in every ministry of the church we should seek to remind people of the soul-soothing effects of our union. Because we are known by God through Christ, we should not fear to come to him. Because we are loved by God through Christ, we should not doubt his presence with us. Because we are adopted into the family of God through Christ, we no longer need to hold on to shame. Much pastoral work should be done through each of these issues, but the bedrock of each affirmation is our union with Christ.

Our union with Christ also shifts our formation from "sin management" to enjoying God and seeking his beauty. When I mentioned the WWJD phenomenon, I thought of all the ways I saw that ethic as simply trying to sin less, rather than enjoy God more. I was focused more on myself and less on the God who redeemed me and set me free from sin. Our desire

---

14. David G. Peterson, *Possessed by God: A New Testament Theology of Sanctification and Holiness* (Downers Grove, IL: IVP Academic, 2001), 114.

to sin less should come from our desire to experience God more. Any environment of formation that focuses simply on sin management to the exclusion of enjoying God will leave people feeling more tired, more ashamed, and more disillusioned. These are exactly the things that our union frees us from! This does not mean we deny the law of God and avoid repentance and growth (more on that in the next chapter), but it does mean we are freed to live for God's glory out of joy instead of fear or selfish gain. When we understand our union with Christ and God's love for us, we can experience our identity and love who we are in Christ.

> **Our desire to sin less should come from our desire to experience God more.**

Last, our union with Christ allows us to truly love ourselves in Christ. You may be asking: "Isn't it wrong to love ourselves?" I would say if we are conceiving of love in the terms of our culture's view of authenticity, then yes. If we are loving ourselves purely for ourselves, then absolutely we should reject it. But for those in Christ, we can now understand the value that God places on us. Though we are not used to this part of the Christian life in our evangelical spirituality, it is a natural consequence of understanding our union. Union with Christ tells us that we are loved by God and allows us to love others and ourselves in light of God's love. To "love your neighbor as yourself" (Matt. 22:39) necessitates reflection on appropriate self-love in relation to God and others. The people who love God and others the best are those who understand their union with Christ the most. Many of our personal issues stem from loving ourselves in the wrong ways, either based on worldly concepts of self-love or ways that neglect the full implications of our union with Christ. In our union with Christ, we become our true selves, and we begin to learn how to love God, love others, and love ourselves in a way that honors God and gives him all the glory.

Final Thoughts

The doctrine of union with Christ, though foundational, may be unfamiliar to you. That's okay. Like Rankin Wilbourne quoted earlier, you may have inherited a different view of how Jesus relates to your spiritual life. There is no lasting and meaningful Christian spiritual formation, however, apart from understanding our union with Christ. For those leading in ministry, your people will not understand their intended direction in the Christian life without you clarifying their union with Christ. I firmly believe that all ministries of the church—whether that be counseling, teaching, preaching, family discipleship, etc.—cannot operate effectively apart from a union-with-Christ framework. Being a child of God in Christ brings hope and a reminder of God's presence with us. David Benner asserts: "There is no true life apart from relationship to God. Therefore there can be no true self apart from this relationship. . . . Any identity that exists apart from this relationship is an illusion."[15] This relationship is secured and flourishes in our union with Christ. In Christ, we have died to

---

15. Benner, *The Gift of Being Yourself*, 83.

the "elements of this world," which lead to "self-made religion" and "false humility" (Col. 2:20–23). Such are the ways of our current culture of authenticity. For God's image-bearers, we have the possibility of something much more: "the new self, the one created according to God's likeness in righteousness and purity of the truth" (Eph. 4:24). In the next chapter, we will explore how that righteousness and purity come about in the process of sanctification.

Resources for Further Study

David G. Benner. *The Gift of Being Yourself: The Sacred Call to Self-Discovery.* Expanded ed. Downers Grove, IL: IVP Books, 2015.

Elyse Fitzpatrick. *Found in Him: The Joy of the Incarnation and Our Union with Christ.* Wheaton, IL: Crossway, 2013.

Marcus Peter Johnson. *One with Christ: An Evangelical Theology of Salvation.* Wheaton, IL: Crossway, 2013.

Robert Letham. *Union with Christ: In Scripture, History, and Theology.* Phillipsburg, NJ: P&R Publishing, 2011.

Rankin Wilbourne. *Union with Christ: The Way to Know and Enjoy God.* Colorado Springs, CO: David C. Cook, 2016.

Questions for Reflection

1. In what ways is union with Christ emphasized in your local church, if at all?

2. Where do you see the current "culture of authenticity" most prevalent?

3. Are there ways that the notion of Gnosticism is present in your church or spiritual formation? How so and to what degree?

4. In what ways do you find your identity in Christ being challenged or questioned? Take a moment to write those down and pray over them, asking God to remind you of the truth of your union with Christ.

5. How might union with Christ help you better understand and appreciate your unique self in spiritual formation?

CHAPTER 4

Getting the Holy Spirit Right for Formation

> Holiness is a most beautiful and lovely thing.
> —JONATHAN EDWARDS[1]

> Holiness is actually the true health of the person.
> Anything else is ugliness and deformity at character level;
> a malfunctioning of the individual; a crippled state of soul.
> —J. I. PACKER[2]

In the 2021 Disney film *Encanto*, the Madrigal family is blessed with special gifts and abilities that help their miraculous Colombian town flourish and thrive. There's one

---

1. Jonathan Edwards, "The Miscellanies" (Entry Nos. a–z, aa–zz, 1–500) in *Works of Jonathan Edwards Online*, vol. 13, ed. Harry S. Stout (Jonathan Edwards Center at Yale University, 2008), 163.

2. J. I. Packer, *Rediscovering Holiness: Knowing the Fullness of Life with God* (Grand Rapids, MI: Baker Books, 2009), 34.

member, however, of the *familia* Madrigal that no one wants to talk about. Though enshrined in family portraits, the whole town knows, "We don't talk about Bruno." Uncle Bruno had the gift of seeing into the future, and all his "tragic" predictions seemed to come true. From dead fish, to spoiled weddings, to balding patterns, Bruno's prophecies—and Bruno himself—had become the town pariah. Rather than trying to understand Bruno, he was simply left unmentioned and dismissed. In the evangelical church today, I feel the Holy Spirit is much like our Uncle Bruno. We know he has gifts and abilities, and he's an integral part of the family, but because we don't understand him (and perhaps we are a little scared of him, if we are being honest), we have decided to leave him out of the picture. The song for *la familia evangélica* might as well be "We Don't Talk about the Spirit."

> **We must not forget that the Spirit is the empowering agent of the church and each individual Christian. To forget or dismiss the Spirit is like pretending your car doesn't have an engine. It's like denying that you need oxygen to survive.**

We must not forget that the Spirit is the empowering agent of the church and each individual Christian. To forget or dismiss the Spirit is like pretending your car doesn't have an engine. It's like denying that you need oxygen to survive. The Spirit truly is the lifeblood of Christian formation. We'll look at two ways in which we need to remember and recover the place and power of the Spirit, particularly regarding Christian spiritual formation. The Spirit undergirds the doctrine of sanctification, or the process of becoming more Christlike in our everyday life. In this chapter, we will briefly explore the person and work of the Spirit to help us understand the role he plays in our formation. This will lead us to consider different ways we respond to the work of Christ and the indwelling Spirit.

Holy Spirit: Who Is He?

As we discussed in chapter 2, the Spirit works inseparably from the Father and Son. Though considered the third member of the Godhead who proceeds from the Father and the Son, he is no less God and no less worthy of worship and honor as God. All such descriptions of the Godhead are never intended to assign value or attempt to dissect the being of God. All three persons are equal in divine nature, power, and will. The Scriptures are unambiguous that the Spirit is God. The Spirit convicts believers of their sin and rebellion (John 16:7–11). The Spirit regenerates, or makes spiritually alive, the believer (John 3:1–8). The Spirit does the work of illuminating the Scriptures (1 Cor. 2:12–15). He also brings assurance (Rom. 8:16), gives spiritual gifts (1 Cor. 12–14), and is the agent that produces Christlikeness (Gal. 5:22–23). According to Paul in Romans 8:11, the Spirit is the one who will give us our resurrection bodies in the new heaven and new earth. Truly, the Spirit does a mighty work!

Too many times, however, we default to fearing the uncomfortable things people do in the name of the Spirit. While this is not a book about how the gifts of the Spirit continue today, all orthodox Christians acknowledge that the Holy Spirit is the third member of the Trinity and has a role to play in the church. Implicitly we know that even if he is not active in the ways he was in the early church, he still has some part to play in our Christian life. For Christian formation to be effective, we need to reestablish a healthy understanding of the Spirit and his vital role to make us more like Christ. And because of that vital role, we need to talk more, sing more, learn more, preach more, and pray more as if the Spirit really is who he says he is and does what he says he'll do.

Sanctification: What Is It?

When talking about the Spirit, we need to understand how it is that the Spirit actually transforms Christians to look more like Jesus. While many doctrines are important for understanding Christian formation (as I hope you have already seen!), perhaps none touches Christian spiritual formation more directly than the doctrine of sanctification. Theologian Gregg Allison defines sanctification as, "The cooperative work of God and Christians by which transformation into greater Christlikeness occurs."[3] Whereas the work of atonement and justification is accomplished completely by God through the person and work of Jesus Christ, the work

---

3. Gregg Allison, "Sanctification" in *The Baker Compact Dictionary of Theological Terms* (Grand Rapids, MI: Baker Books, 2016), 196.

of sanctification is a collaborative effort. Paul's words to the church set the tone for sanctification: "Therefore, my dear friends, just as you have always obeyed, so now, not only in my presence but even more in my absence, work out your own salvation with fear and trembling. For it is God who is working in you both to will and to work according to his good purpose" (Phil. 2:12–13). We work knowing that God works in us. Our salvation is secured, but Christians now partner with the Holy Spirit to discover and apply all the riches of Christ's work on our behalf. Because the love of God has been poured forth in our hearts (Rom. 5:5), we have the ability and desire to grow in godliness and Christlike virtue. With redeemed hearts and transformed minds (Rom. 12:2), we gain a new perspective on the utter ugliness of sin and the staggering beauty of the triune God. This is the journey and joy of sanctification.

Traditionally, the doctrine of sanctification has been understood to comprise two complimentary parts. The first part of sanctification is what theologians describe as *definite* or *positional* sanctification. In this aspect of sanctification God sets believers apart from nonbelievers. This is the basic idea of being "holy." In this way, we have been "washed" and "sanctified" (1 Cor. 6:11); we have been made "dead to sin" (Rom. 6:11); and we have been "crucified with Christ" (Gal. 2:20). These deep realities are forever true for Christians, thus being "definite" or "accomplished" once and for all. This is why the New Testament calls us "saints." Sainthood is not earned, it is conferred. We are set apart for God's kingdom, given a new identity in Christ, and gifted with the Holy Spirit to live in a new way.

Sanctification is also *progressive.* This is the active growth that proceeds from a life of faith in Jesus Christ. The imperatives of the New Testament, to one degree or another, are reminders to walk in the Spirit as part of our progressive sanctification. Though we are saints, we are now called to live out that saintly identity. When Christians think of sanctification, most likely they think of progressive sanctification. The progressive understanding of sanctification fuels the active part of the Christian life, and it is supremely important to pursue holy living. But we need to also remember that we have the identity of a saint. Like Paul greeting the saints gathered at Corinth, pastors and ministry leaders should greet the saints gathered in Fort Worth, Texas, or Riverside, California, or Lyons, France. We are saints who are in the process of becoming saintlier. We must maintain our positional sanctification while encouraging our progress in holiness. In fact, when we neglect one or the other, our sanctification can run off the rails. Let's explore this in more detail.

Models of Sanctification

While the doctrine of sanctification has been pivotal to the Christian life since the beginning, the "how" of sanctification has been debated throughout the centuries.[4] What we believe about sanctification and how it happens matters a great deal. A deficient and incomplete view of sanctification

---

4. For a helpful overview of specific models of sanctification, see Andy Naseli, "Models of Sanctification," The Gospel Coalition, https://www.thegospelcoalition.org/essay/models-of-sanctification/.

will lead to deficient and incomplete disciples. David Powilson has said, "Sanctification is a journey, not a destination. The real key is the direction you're heading, not the distance you've traveled or the place you've reached."[5] There are different ways that people have mapped out that journey throughout the history of the church. I could write an entire book on the history of sanctification, including important names and events; instead, I want you to see how sanctification has been related to justification and the effects of

> A deficient and incomplete view of sanctification will lead to deficient and incomplete disciples.

getting that relationship out of balance. I will highlight three options for us to consider and how they each impact Christian formation in different ways.

Option 1: Sanctification = Justification

In some views of sanctification, the lines between sanctification and justification (or our right standing before God based on the work of Christ) are severely blurred. So much so, that works done for God are seen as necessary to contribute to our salvation. This general view sees the words of Paul in Philippians 2:12–13 as meaning that our salvation

---

5. David Powlison, "Play the Long Game of Sanctification," The Gospel Coalition, https://www.thegospelcoalition.org/article/play-the-long-game-of-sanctification/.

is ultimately dependent upon us. Rather than working out our salvation based upon the finished work of Christ, we are working *for* our salvation. Christ only made salvation *possible*, and it's up to us to finish the process. Like putting money in an investment account, every good work is a deposit toward a hopeful return. There is always fear that we have not done enough, always thinking we could be doing better and receiving almost no assurance in our spiritual walk. Every downturn in the economy of our spiritual life leads to a state of spiritual depression. Can we ever make up the difference? Will we ever be able to get back on top? Will the scales ever tip in our favor? There are always plenty of questions and few satisfactory answers. Christian formation devolves into doing things for God without a joy or satisfaction in the things of God.

I suspect that most nominal Christians have this view of Christian formation. It's also the way most non-Christians perceive religious life in general. However, it's a gross mischaracterization of the Christian life that has left many unable (or unwilling) to pursue healthy Christian spiritual formation. For those who do persevere in this mindset, the temptation toward pride, envy, or bitterness lurks around every corner of good works. Because this is a deficient view of the Christian life, adherents have to either redefine the Christian life completely or else create a web of self-justifications for why they—with their perceived good works—are enough to merit salvation. Friends, let me put this in the strongest terms possible: this is *NOT* the Christian life. This is not what Christ has called his people into. It is not the vision of Christian formation woven throughout the Scriptures. This version of the Christian life lacks joy in the work of Christ, shifts our view to ourselves rather than God's glory and splendor, and removes almost any opportunity for true humility and Spirit-driven fruitfulness. I am *not* saying that there may not be genuine and well-meaning Christians who have this view of the Christian life, but I would unhesitatingly argue that their Christian formation is insufficient. They persevere in the Christian life despite this mode of formation, not because of it.

Another way this view of sanctification plays out is the incessant need for "spiritual experiences" to ensure that one is advancing in spiritual formation. Even more so, such experiences usually have to be intensely emotional to be true and meaningful for one's spiritual life. Experiences such as retreats, special times of worship, and other activities within the church are a vital part of the Christian life. They can enrich one's formation and provide a time of refreshment and renewed vigor in the Christian life. They cannot, however, be the sole means of how we grow in our spirituality. Nor can we gauge the effectiveness of such activities based on our emotional experience. The Christian life is not always a life of exuberant victory and mountaintop experiences. When our sanctification is reduced to such experiences, we are left with a Christian spiritual formation that is dependent upon the movement of a song chorus rather than movement of the Spirit. We also tend to neglect the ways the Spirit may be forming us in times of trial or suffering, even believing that such events are contrary to the "victorious" Christian life. We believe the lie that God only wants to bring us success, fulfillment, and happiness (defined in worldly terms), and that anything contrary cannot possibly be from God. I fear that this is where many evangelical Christians find themselves. While this may not seem like legalistic or works-based formation, there is no other way to describe it. If growth is dependent upon spiritual and emotional experiences, then once again the focus remains on us and our ability to conjure up "good vibes" in the midst of smoke and lasers rather than gospel fruit forged in the trials of everyday life.

Please know that I don't have a particular denomination, Christian tradition, or specific church in mind. It's important to mention here that this is not an "us versus them" argument. While it may be easy for us to shake our fists at others, all Christians should do a regular check in the mirror to make sure the fist-shaking is going in the right direction. The default mode of our heart is to justify ourselves, assume our works are necessary at some level to complete our salvation, and generally assume the Christian life is about all that *we* are doing for the Lord. So, while some traditions may have this idea of sanctification more firmly embedded, no one is immune to the alluring effects of "good works" Christianity.

C. S. Lewis beautifully illustrated this in his *Screwtape Letters*, a fictional correspondence between a senior demon and his subordinate. Screwtape tells his understudy Wormwood not to worry now that the "patient" has become a Christian. He states: "What he says, even on his knees, about his own sinfulness is all parrot talk. At bottom, he still believes he has run up a very favourable credit-balance in the Enemy's ledger by allowing himself to be converted, and thinks that he is showing great humility and condescension in going to church with these 'smug', commonplace neighbours at all. Keep him in that state of mind as long as you can."[6] The "Enemy" from their point of view is God, and these fictional demons know just how to get into the heart and mind of their patients so as to distract them away from the transforming power of the gospel. The real Wormwoods have greatly succeeded at accomplishing this task. This view of sanctification is clearly deficient, but what other sanctification options do Christians have?

Option 2: Justification > Sanctification

If one side of the spectrum is to equate our sanctification with our justification, therefore seeking to earn our salvation, the other side almost obliterates sanctification altogether. In this view, the most important side of the Christian life is our justification. It is a gospel of merely sin forgiveness rather than total life transformation. This is the version of the Christian life that focuses upon the indicatives of the gospel to the neglect of the imperatives. But let's be fair. The indicatives, the propositional and timeless truths about the gospel, are medicine for the weary soul. We should never tire of hearing that there is "now no condemnation for those in Christ Jesus" (Rom. 8:1), that we have been made "alive with Christ even though we were dead in trespasses" (Eph. 2:5), and that Christ "suffered for sins once for all" (1 Pet. 3:18). These are the good gospel promises that our faith, hope, and love rest

---

6. C. S. Lewis, *The Screwtape Letters* (New York, NY: HarperOne, 2009), 8–9.

upon. But all these foundational truths have corresponding commitments. Because there is no longer any condemnation, we can set our minds "on the things of the Spirit" rather than "the things of the flesh" (Rom. 8:5). Because we have been made alive in Christ, we can walk in the "good works, which God prepared ahead of time for us to do" (Eph. 2:10). And because our sins have been forgiven once and for all through Christ's work, we live "no longer for human desires, but for God's will" (1 Pet. 4:2). So clearly our justification is pivotal, but it is not the end of the story. The Christian life is not just getting used to our justification, it is recognizing the grace and mercy which made our justification possible and submitting to the call of holiness.[7]

The view that focuses exclusively on our justification to the neglect of our sanctification has come to be known as antinomianism, or "against the law." This way of Christian formation tends to neglect good works, eschew striving for holiness, and downplay actively killing sin in one's life. The term and idea have roots in the Protestant Reformation, when various figures falsely accused Martin Luther and his followers of denying the moral demands of the Christian life due to their emphasis on justification by faith alone.[8] While there may have been some who went this direction, Protestant

---

7. The notion of sanctification as "getting used to our justification" comes from Gerhard O. Forde, "The Lutheran View" in Donald L. Alexander, ed., *Christian Spirituality: Five Views of Sanctification* (Downers Grove, IL: IVP Academic, 1989).

8. Sinclair Ferguson, *The Whole Christ: Legalism, Antinomianism, and Gospel Assurance—Why the Marrow Controversy Still Matters* (Wheaton, IL: Crossway, 2016), 138. Ferguson's book is a helpful resource to understand the historical and practical issues related to antinomianism.

Reformers were anything but antinomian. Mark Jones, in his work on antinomianism, sums up this view of the Christian life: "[A]ntinomians . . . rejected the idea that the law, accompanied by the Spirit, is a true means of sanctification."[9] God's instructions for godly living are meant to produce godly results. To neglect them, or deny them completely, is detrimental to one's spiritual health. Christian formation in this view focuses upon the grace of God apart from the moral and practical ways that grace intends to transform us. This is exactly what Paul was addressing in Romans 6 when he said, "Should we continue in sin so that grace may multiply? Absolutely not! How can we who died to sin still live in it?" (Rom. 6:1–2). Biblical scholar Doug Moo, commenting on this passage, observes: "Paul argues that the law could never curb sinning; and the reign of grace, far from encouraging sin, is the only means by which sin can truly be defeated."[10] Grace is the power by which we fight sin. Grace is the way in which we see sin for what it is: an offense to a holy and just God. Grace is not just a "get out of jail free" card. Nor is grace a means to continue doing what we want. Grace is an opportunity to step into a life of more freedom, a freedom to live beautiful lives in the pursuit of holiness. Those who are serious about Christian spiritual formation will never tire of preaching, teaching, singing, and talking about grace—but they will never do so in contrast to holiness. Grace enables one, not excuses one, to live a holy life.

---

9. Mark Jones, *Antinomianism: Reformed Theology's Unwelcome Guest* (Phillipsburg, NJ: P&R Books, 2013), 125.

10. Douglas J. Moo, *The Epistle to the Romans*, The New International Commentary on the New Testament (Grand Rapids, MI: Wm. B. Eerdmans, 1996), 356.

There is much more we could say about Christian spiritual formation that neglects the grace-driven, Holy Spirit–filled, striving in holiness. Like option one, there are certainly many well-meaning and genuine believers who have been formed in this way. They value grace, and that's not a bad thing! But grace to the neglect of holiness devalues grace. Many people have found freedom in churches which prioritize grace, but they eventually drown because they miss the safe harbor of holiness that grace points to. Formation that gives us nothing to do in light of grace will create "rocky ground" disciples, those whom Jesus described as receiving the gospel with joy but who eventually wither when distress and persecution come their way (Matt. 13:20–21). Like option-one disciples, these disciples have only received one side of the gospel. For spiritual formation to flourish in the life of the church, disciples need to know both the indicative truths and the imperative commands. So, what is another way?

> For spiritual formation to flourish in the life of the church, disciples need to know both the indicative truths and the imperative commands.

Option 3: Justification therefore Sanctification

While some want to conflate justification with sanctification, and others want to erase sanctification entirely, what are we left with? Both doctrinal categories of justification and sanctification are vital for understanding the Christian faith and how it plays out in our spiritual life. Therefore, for spiritual formation to be meaningful, Christians need to see how their justification leads to sanctification. You can't have one without the other. Sanctification begins at the moment of conversion and continues for a lifetime. Sixteenth-century reformer John Calvin summarizes this beautifully: "Christ justifies no one whom he does not at the same time sanctify. These benefits are joined together by an everlasting and indissoluble bond."[11] Elsewhere Calvin makes a similar, if not more drastic, observation: "Justification and sanctification, gifts of grace, go together as if tied by an inseparable bond, so that if anyone tries to separate them, he is, in a sense, tearing Christ to pieces."[12]

To understand this more clearly, once again Gregg Allison helps us here. He states: "Unlike other divine works, which are monergistic (God alone works), sanctification is synergistic. God operates in ways that are proper to his divine agency (e.g., convicting of sin, empowering by the Spirit, willing and working to accomplish his good pleasure), and Christians work in ways that are proper to their human agency (e.g., reading Scripture, praying, mortifying sin, yielding to the Spirit)."[13] God has done the work of justification, something we could never accomplish, but now he invites us into the life of the Spirit and calls us to live a transformed life based on the person and work of Jesus Christ. We are in Christ by faith,

---

11. John Calvin, *Institutes of the Christian Religion*, 3.16.1
12. John Calvin, *Calvin's Commentary on 1 Corinthians 1:30*.
13. Allison, "Sanctification," 196.

and he is in us by the power of the Spirit. Justification leads to sanctification and establishes the best way to understand Christian spiritual formation.

Along with Paul in Romans 6, the apostle James helps us understand this dynamic between our justification and sanctification. After summarizing the works of Abraham and Rahab as a demonstration of their faith, he concludes: "For just as the body without the spirit is dead, so also faith without works is dead" (James 2:26). Faith is the engine that drives the vehicle of our Christian life. It's the fuel for our spirituality. It's the vital supplement our piety needs to grow stronger and flourish. Our works are to be an expression of gratitude for salvation, as Paul confirms in Ephesians 2:10. Another way to understand this is that sanctification is part recognizing that our redemption has been accomplished by Christ, and part realizing that our redemption is being applied by the Spirit.[14]

Sanctification Pitfalls to Avoid

When I was in college, I took several photography classes. I'm not talking about how to use a digital camera, as good of a skill as that is. This was about developing film, spending

---

14. This way of describing our sanctification comes from the classic work of John Murray, *Redemption Accomplished and Applied,* rev. ed. (Grand Rapids, MI: Wm. B. Eerdmans, 2015). Regarding sanctification, Murray states: "The believer is not yet so conformed to the image of Christ that he is holy, harmless, undefiled, and separate from sinners. Sanctification is concerned precisely with this fact and it has as its aim the elimination of all sin and complete conformation to the image of God's own Son, to be holy as the Lord is holy" (page 152).

hours in dark rooms, and splashing dangerous chemicals all over myself. Everything had to be meticulously orchestrated, timed, and executed to develop the film you needed and the prints you wanted. A miscalculation or a fit of impatience could cost you precious time and money. I remember once rushing to complete a project (likely due to my own procrastination), and the prints showed it. They were underdeveloped, too gray (this was a black-and-white photography class), and overall, just flat. My professor could tell that I had not put in the time needed to produce the best prints possible. I rushed the process and paid the price with my grade. When it comes to the work of sanctification by the power of the Spirit, it can be tempting to rush the process. We want quick results, and in the end, we likely develop flat and gray disciples. While definitive sanctification is instantaneous, progressive sanctification is slow. Sanctification is not about perfection but persistence, because fighting sin is a lifelong endeavor. There is no insta-sanctification or seven steps to become successfully sanctified in seven days. So the first pitfall to avoid is simply our impatience. There are moments where growth happens quickly, but the overall trajectory of our sanctification is a long journey.

The second pitfall to avoid is neglecting the role of suffering in our sanctification. This aspect of our Christian life is rarely discussed and often dismissed in evangelicalism. Still, suffering and persecution are inevitable for "all who want to live a godly life in Christ Jesus" (2 Tim. 3:12). Suffering is also a part of God's calling for his disciples if we take the words of Jesus in Luke 9:23 seriously. This is not because God has ill intentions toward us, but simply that the life of Christ is

contrary to the way of the world and that God will redeem
and use suffering for his purposes and our growth. In Romans
8:28, Paul ensures that suffering and trials are never without
purposes in God's economy. This doesn't mean we can explain
or understand all the reasons suffering happens, but they never
escape God's notice or his sovereignty. And as James encourages the church, suffering produces endurance so that we "may
be mature and complete, lacking nothing" (James 1:2–4).
Sanctification is meant to increase our dependence upon the
Lord and further produce in us faith, hope, and love. It instills
in our hearts our longing to behold his beauty and the resto-
ration of all things in Christ. Thus, suffering and trials play a
major role in our sanctification. When we try to explain away
trials or pretend that suffering doesn't exist, we stifle spiritual
formation and disregard the providence of God.

The next pitfall to avoid is thinking that sanctification is
solely a personal project. God has equipped the church through
the power of the Spirit to be a place of corporate sanctification and formation. We need each other to grow collectively
and individually into the image of Christ. Sanctification is
both highly personal and deeply communal. There is no such
thing as a growing Christian apart from an active life in the
body of Christ. Christians are called into a body, a group of
other believers, to experience the work of the Spirit in our
lives together. In fact, evidence that our sanctification is taking place is that we consider others' needs greater than our
own. Paul tells the Galatians, "Carry one another's burdens; in
this way you will fulfill the law of Christ" (Gal. 6:2). Timothy
George, commenting on this verse, illustrates it well by saying,

"The church of Jesus Christ is not a charitable organization like the Red Cross or a civic club such as the Rotary or Kiwanis. It is rather a family of born-again brothers and sisters supernaturally knit together by the Holy Spirit in a common fellowship of mutual edification and love."[15] The law of Christ is self-sacrificial love. If we don't have "another" around us to love and care for, it would be impossible to do what Christ calls us to. As we discussed in a previous chapter, the Christian life is communal because God is triune. Therefore, we are most fulfilled as Christians when in community with others. When considering the ways spiritual formation can and should take place within the church, we must never forget that our formation is a community venture.

The final pitfall is to assume one size fits all for sanctification. When we understand the profound nature of our union with Jesus, then we begin to see the immense riches available to us for our growth in godliness. Thus, sanctification is multifaceted and meets every one of us exactly where we are on our journey of becoming more like our Savior. Though they may be similar, no two roads of sanctification are exactly alike. We are unique human beings who have been affected by the Fall in unique ways. Even though we all suffer from the same disease, our symptoms are often different. We all need the Great Physician, but his remedies are as unique as the ones whom he created. Though sanctification is deeply personal, we must remember that the Alpha and Omega of sanctification is Christ himself. The first spark of justifying faith sets us

---

15. Timothy George, *Galatians*, The New American Commentary, vol. 30 (Nashville, TN: Broadman & Holman Publishers, 1994), 413.

apart as "holy ones" of God and simultaneously lights the first flame of our growth in Christlikeness. All tributaries of the Spirit's subjective application of Jesus's objective work flow into this one source: to know, enjoy, delight in, and adore Jesus Christ for all time.

In his book, *How Does Sanctification Work?*, David Powlison gives us five factors toward our sanctification:

1. **God:** "It is God who works in you, both to will and to work for his good pleasure" (Phil. 2:13 ESV).

2. **Truth:** The truth of God's Word taught, sung, preached, studied, and read is one of the surest means by which the Spirit brings about change in our lives.

3. **Wise people:** God mediates our change "through the gifts and graces of brothers and sisters in Christ."

4. **Suffering and struggles:** Though we don't relish it, suffering and struggles work toward our growth in Christlikeness. Difficulties prompt us to rely on God. Writes Powlison: "People change because something is hard, not because it goes well . . . Struggles force us to need God."

5. **You change:** Scripture calls us to actively believe, obey, trust, seek, love, confess, praise, and take refuge. We are not passive. The mystery of faith is that we are

100-percent responsible, yet 100-percent dependent on outside help.[16]

How these factors play out in each of our lives may look drastically different. The Spirit is at work, applying the objective work of Christ, yet that work touches us all differently. While journeying toward the same goal, each believer will have a distinct path which they will tread.

Final Thoughts

In his classic book, *Holiness*, the nineteenth-century Anglican bishop J. C. Ryle conjectured: "What could an unsanctified man do in heaven, if by any chance he got there? . . . No man can possibly be happy in a place where he is not in his element and where all around him is not congenial to his taste, habits, and character."[17] Ryle understood the point of sanctification: to form Christians into the character and likeness of Christ. Those who have not been transformed by the Spirit would not feel at home in heaven. The task of sanctification *is* the task of formation: forming one's habits and character with an eye toward eternity. A proper understanding of sanctification is vital for a thriving Christian life both now and in the age to come. Those of us who have been walking with Christ for any length of time recognize that the work of sanctification is slow. There is no insta-sanctification.

---

16. David Powlison, *How Does Sanctification Work?* (Wheaton, IL: Crossway, 2017), 63–67.

17. J. C. Ryle, *Holiness: Its Nature, Hindrances, Difficulties, and Roots* (Grand Rapids, MI: Christian Classics Ethereal Library, 2017), 34.

There are many twists and turns. It's also deeply personal as we each have different areas of life in which the Spirit is working. Sanctification is a highly corporate project as well. The "us" of sanctification is just as important as the "I" within the Christian life. Lest you think sanctification is simply an exercise in theological research, hear the words of noted theologian Sinclair Ferguson: "Of all the doctrines surrounding the Christian life this, one of the profoundest, is also one of the most practical in its effects."[18]

Resources for Further Study

Jerry Bridges. *Transforming Grace*. Colorado Springs, CO: NavPress, 2008.

Sinclair B. Ferguson. *The Holy Spirit: Contours of Christian Theology*. Downers Grove, IL: IVP Academic, 1997.

J. I. Packer. *Keep in Step with the Spirit*. Wheaton, IL: Crossway, 2021.

———. *Rediscovering Holiness: Knowing the Fullness of Life with God*. Wheaton, IL: Crossway, 2021.

David Powlison. *How Does Sanctification Work?* Wheaton, IL: Crossway, 2017.

---

18. Sinclair Ferguson, *The Christian Life: A Doctrinal Introduction* (Edinburgh, UK: Banner of Truth, 2013), 114.

Questions for Reflection

1. In what ways does your local church emphasize the role of the Spirit? If it doesn't, what might be the reasons?

2. Read Galatians 5:22–26. What are the ways in which living in the Spirit is described here?

3. Reflect again on Galatians 5:22–26. Which virtues or fruit of the Spirit do you wish to cultivate more in your life?

4. Of the different "options" given for understanding sanctification, which one have you adhered to most in your life? What have been the effects in your Christian formation?

5. In what areas of your life are you wishing to see further sanctification? If in a group and feeling comfortable, take a moment to share those and ask for prayer and accountability. If alone, write them down and pray over them, while considering how the Lord may be calling you to holiness and growth in those areas.

PART 2

Practical Foundations
for Christian Formation

CHAPTER 5

Formation of the Corporate Body

Let the word of Christ dwell richly among you, in all
wisdom teaching and admonishing one another through
psalms, hymns, and spiritual songs, singing to God with
gratitude in your hearts.
—COLOSSIANS 3:16

It is the fellowship of the cross to experience the burden
of the other. If one does not experience it, the fellowship
he belongs to is not Christian.
—DIETRICH BONHOEFFER[1]

N ow that we have established the key theological foundations for formation, it's time we begin connecting the
doctrinal dots to the practical ones. So when you think of the

---

1. Dietrich Bonhoeffer, *Life Together: The Classic Exploration of
Christian Community* (New York: Harper One, 1954), 101.

practice of spiritual formation, what comes to mind? If you're like me, the first place I go is to personal practices and disciplines of the Christian spiritual life. This is certainly an important aspect of Christian formation and discipleship. We need to cultivate godly habits and personal holiness, but they are only meaningful insofar as they are connected to a corporate gathering of Christ-followers. We can only gauge our growth in godliness effectively in connection with others. For spiritual formation to be meaningful and faithful to Scripture, we must prioritize and cultivate biblically meaningful corporate formation practices. The life of the body of Christ should feed and enhance our personal spiritual life. Our churches will form healthy disciples insofar as they take the corporate gathering seriously. If your church does not prioritize the gathering as indispensable to spiritual formation, you need to ask why.

Every church does formation. Every church has a liturgy. Every church has a ministry emphasis. The question is whether one's formation is biblical and thriving, or not. By walking through the foyer, observing your worship center, and reviewing your calendar of events, I can tell you pretty quickly what your church formation and discipleship priorities are. Some may place a heavy emphasis on evangelism and inviting unbelievers to church. Others might place a high priority on expositing the text of Scripture as the main event of worship. Still others might give more attention to music performance and production.

None of these are bad. We need evangelistic cultures. We need sound preaching. We need meaningful worship. What happens, however, is that we often create environments centered on one to the exclusion or devaluation of the others. For effective spiritual formation in the church, we must maintain a balanced approach. If the priority is evangelism and conversions, we can move toward a seeker-sensitive environment that waters down doctrine and devalues liturgy. If the priority is preaching, we can move toward forsaking other avenues of discipleship. If the priority falls on excellence in worship, we can move toward Sunday morning as a performance and manufactured emotional experience. What we emphasize most in the gathering tends to color and affect everything else we do in church. For Christian spiritual formation to thrive, we must view the corporate gathering and the activities of the local church as indispensable. We must also see every activity as an opportunity to form disciples to experience the goodness of God, engage the truth of God, and encounter the beauty of God together.

Why the Church?

Why is the church necessary and how does God use the church for his purposes and our growth? Theologian Christopher Morgan states that "[the] Bible's emphasis is on the church as a group of believers committed to Christ and one another, working together to glorify God and fulfill his mission."[2] God has called out a people, those united to Christ by grace through faith and placed in the body of Christ for the purpose of becoming more like Christ and proclaiming the

---

2. Christopher W. Morgan, "Church" in *A Concise Dictionary of Theological Terms* (Nashville, TN: B&H Academic, 2020), 31.

name of Christ. God works to sanctify us through other people. We work together for the glory of God and the good of one another. The New Testament picture is one of ongoing gatherings for the sake of sharing, encouraging, and bearing others' burdens (see Acts 2:42; Gal. 6:1–6). The local church is the locus of Christ's body (including his members) and the place where the Spirit works (see 1 Cor. 3:16, 12:27).

The church also displays the creative genius of God in knitting a people together from "every nation, tribe, people, and language" (Rev. 7:9). In this way, he is using what the world doesn't expect—a group of ordinary people who would not normally gather—to accomplish his work. It shows that God chooses "what is foolish in the world to shame the wise" and that he chooses "what is weak in the world to shame the strong" (1 Cor. 1:27). The church is where the gospel is both proclaimed and lived out. We proclaim the power of God both for salvation and for sustaining our Christian life.

> The community of Christ is where the Spirit dwells and is at work. When we get together in fellowship with one another, we experience the gifts of the Spirit and the work of the Spirit through the means of grace appointed for the church.

James Wilhoit describes this gospel reality perfectly: "The gospel is the power of God for the beginning, middle,

and the end of salvation. It is not what we need to proclaim to unbelievers; the gospel also needs to permeate our entire Christian experience."[3] The church is the primary place where we are formed into gospel people. We center our time, our worship, our fellowship and more on the resurrected Jesus Christ. Michael Svigel and Nathan Holsteen add a helpful point: "The community is definitely Son-centered, and it's also Spirit-formed. The Holy Spirit of God forms the church of Jesus Christ."[4] The community of Christ is where the Spirit dwells and is at work. When we get together in fellowship with one another, we experience the gifts of the Spirit and the work of the Spirit through the means of grace appointed for the church. So this leads us to consider what the means of grace in the church actually are. What do the "means" mean?

Corporate Means of Grace

In his book *Habits of Grace*, David Mathis describes disciplines or habits of the Christian life as ways in which we intentionally put ourselves in the pathway of God's grace. They are the tangible means, or ways, we experience God's grace. He states: "The means of grace fill our tank for the pursuit of joy, for the good of others, and for the glory of God. . . . they are blessings—not mere disciplines, but channels through

---

3. James C. Wilhoit, *Spiritual Formation as if the Church Matters: Growing in Christ Through Community*, 2nd ed.(Grand Rapids, MI: Baker Academic, 2022), 17.

4. Nathan D. Holsteen and Michael J. Svigel, *Exploring Christian Theology, vol. 3: The Church, Spiritual Growth, and the End Times* (Bloomington, MN: Bethany House Publishers, 2014), 27.

which God gives us spiritual food for our survival, growth, and flourishing in the mission."[5] Whatever godly habit, practice, or experience that causes us to encounter God's grace and promises to us in Christ, is a means of grace. As Christians we confess that God is the "God of all grace" (1 Pet. 5:10) and from Christ we have received "grace upon grace" (John 1:16). We proclaim that we are "saved by grace through faith, and this is not from yourselves; it is God's gift—not from works, so that no one can boast" (Eph. 2:8–9). By grace we are increasingly "conformed to the image of his Son" (Rom. 8:29). The means of grace, therefore, is any practice that helps you remember and relish the grace you have received (and continue to receive) from God.

It is important to remember that the means of grace point to Jesus. In the habits of the Christian life, Jesus is always the goal. The habits of our corporate gathering should always leave people refreshed by the work of Christ more than the work of a preacher or praise band. As Christians, we affirm God uses ordinary things to communicate extraordinary truth. Whether it be a paper napkin to share the gospel, a hug to show a tangible expression of God's love, a three-chord progression to communicate Trinitarian doctrine, or the bread and wine (or juice) in the Lord's Supper to confess Christ's atonement, we use common items to share remarkable things. The truth and power of God's Word is what gives ordinary things weight and substance. The Spirit of God uses the Word of God to form and develop the people of God. Formation

---

5. David Mathis, *Habits of Grace: Enjoying Jesus through the Spiritual Disciplines* (Wheaton, IL: Crossway, 2016), 32.

is primarily by the Word and through the Spirit. When we consider the habits of the local church, we need to ensure that each one is undergirded by the power and authority of God's Word. Without God's Word and Spirit there is no grace, only means—and means without grace is dead.

Let's look more closely at the "essential" means of grace that must be present for local churches to form healthy and thriving disciples of Christ.

Essential Means 1: The Word through Speech

Corporate formation begins with a dedication to greeting one another, sharing God's grace with Word-centered encouragement and conversation with one another. As Paul exhorted believers in Rome to live in unity and serve one another, he encouraged them to "pursue what promotes peace and what builds up one another" (Rom. 14:19). Your church experience may have been anything but an exercise in building up others. It seems that much of the church (especially on social media) is more prone to "bite and devour one another" (Gal. 5:15). Christians, however, must consider how to be for the good of the other. Being for another's good begins with building up others and greeting one another. While most of us may not practice the "holy kiss" described in Scripture (see 2 Cor. 13:12), we would do well to greet and welcome one another in that Spirit—embracing one another as a sign of our common faith, hope, and love.

Our speech in corporate formation should also include numerous opportunities for the Word to "dwell richly among [us]" (Col. 3:16). While Paul appears to link this primarily to worship through song, he concludes with an all-inclusive: "And whatever you do, in word or in deed, do everything in the name of the Lord Jesus, giving thanks to God the Father through him" (v. 17). Christian spiritual formation prioritizes the Word in every vista and venue of corporate life. From our call to worship, to our time of confession, to closing announcements, how does the Word of God permeate everything we do in worship? We will never fail if we include more Scripture in our worship rather than less. This includes reading as much Scripture as possible in Sunday worship and other corporate gatherings. Paul's instruction to Timothy should be taken with the utmost seriousness: "[Give] your attention to public reading, exhortation, and teaching" (1 Tim. 4:13). Too often the only time we hear Scripture read in worship is during the sermon, and sometimes that's not guaranteed! Giving priority to the regular reading of Scripture in corporate worship will bring the Word alive in fresh ways and contribute to increasing the biblical literacy of the people. While some traditions use Scripture lectionaries to provide an order of passages, it can be as simple as choosing passages that coincide with the sermon's theme or tapping into widely available Bible reading plans. Whatever the method, those serious about corporate formation should always err on the side of more Scripture in worship, not less.

A last reminder on our speech and communication with one another: people are watching. Jesus said that others will know that we are his disciples by the love we show one another (John 13:35). We may need to have tough conversations in church, but this does not mean we should give up speaking "truth in love" (Eph. 4:15). When we speak truth without love, our language can become insensitive and even abusive. When we speak love without truth, we can end up giving license to sin and immorality. Both are contrary to the gospel and negate our Christian witness. Therefore, our speech should "always be gracious, seasoned with salt" (Col. 4:6). The way we speak to each other in the church has a direct impact on our witness to the world. We need to develop a habit of grace-filled speech that includes edification, exhortation, and encouragement (see 1 Thess. 4:18, 5:11; Heb. 3:13). When we lose the ability to speak well of one another and forgo the desire to "[take] the lead in honoring one another" (Rom. 12:10), we not only lose traction in our Christian formation, but we lose purchase with a lost and dying world. Our words matter, and as Dan Darling notes: "Words can create or destroy, they can uplift or condemn. They can reflect the Word by which God has spoken or they can echo the whispers of the serpent."[6] If people are not encouraged, exhorted, and edified with the Word, then other corporate formation practices will fall upon deaf ears and hard hearts.

Essential Means 2: The Word through Song

I grew up in a church that took Ephesians 5:19 and Colossians 3:16 very seriously. So seriously, in fact, that the only type of worship allowed in the church was *a cappella* (i.e., no instruments). There is nothing intrinsically wrong with

---

6. Daniel Darling, *A Way with Words: Using Our Online Conversations for Good* (Nashville, TN: B&H Publishing Group, 2020), 14.

worshiping only with voices. In fact, vocal-only worship can help remove some of the distraction and performance-driven music in evangelical worship today. For the record, I'm fully on board with guitars and drums in worship. Even as a kid I remembered scratching my head at the fact that we sold the latest worship cassette (and eventually CDs) in our church bookstore. If Sunday morning was voices-only, why was it okay to listen to instrumental worship on your own time? The inconsistency was taken to the next level when I attended a university within my former church tradition that only brought live musicians to campus so long as they weren't playing worship music. Very strange indeed. Songs, hymns, and spiritual songs are instrument-less. Full stop.

While I no longer adhere to this theological tradition, it is a good and godly thing to encourage one another with song, even if you choose to do so *a cappella*. Corporate worship, whatever the mode, is intended to bring great comfort and godly conviction. This happens when songs are directly connected to the truth of God's Word. Whether backed by a guitar riff or an alto voice, corporate formation includes reminding each other of the gospel message through song. Paul records two of the earliest hymns of the church in Colossians 1:15–20 and Philippians 2:5–11. These works contained the entire gospel story in hymn form. From Creation, Fall, redemption,

> Corporate worship, whatever the mode, is intended to bring great comfort and godly conviction.

and consummation, our songs must allow disciples to sing and confess the entire narrative of God's Word.

Mike Cosper contends: "The goal of our gatherings should be to cultivate practices that form our church to live in the good news of the gospel. . . . Nothing better prepares us for life's ups and downs, humbles and affirms us, roots us in where we are, and points us to where we're going."[7] If our worship veers more toward victory in Jesus, we lose the right expression of lament and loss in the face of sin and brokenness. If we only focus on the depravity of humanity, we miss the hope found in Jesus. Corporate formation includes singing about the realities of our struggles *and* the hope of God's presence and abiding love. We sing out with the psalmist, "God is our refuge and strength, a helper who is always found in times of trouble" (Ps. 46:1). We find solace as we sing that "there is now no condemnation for those in Christ Jesus" (Rom. 8:1). All these beautiful truths and more are the foundation for Word-centered worship in the church. The best corporate worship weaves the thread of the gospel all throughout. Cosper observes: "Liturgy that immerses the people of God in the rhythms of grace doesn't merely train them for

> **Prioritize the Word in worship and you will have disciples who prioritize the Word in their hearts.**

---

7. Mike Cosper, *Rhythms of Grace: How the Church's Worship Tells the Story of the Gospel* (Wheaton, IL: Crossway, 2013), 121.

gospel-centered worship; it trains them for gospel-centered lives."[8] Prioritize the Word in worship and you will have disciples who prioritize the Word in their hearts.

Essential Means 3: The Word through Sermon

Many of us consider the sermon *the* event of Sunday morning. Since the Reformation, the regular exposition of God's Word has been the central facet of Christian worship in the Protestant tradition. I am not about to argue that it should change. What I do fear, however, is that this central component of worship has led to devaluing other aspects of corporate formation. We have already discussed our speech, the need for consistent public reading of Scripture, and the necessity of songs saturated with Scripture. Faithful preaching of the Word is built upon, and feeds into, other corporate practices. Preaching, though central, is just one component of our worship. If we rush through worship to get to the sermon, we deny what Scripture says we are to do when we gather, and stifle spiritual formation in the body of Christ.

Yet, corporate spiritual formation must include the regular exposition of Scripture. Paul tells Timothy unequivocally: "Preach the word." This act of preaching and teaching includes correction and rebuking, as well as encouragement "with great patience" (2 Tim. 4:2). The call to preach is a call to bring the Scriptures to bear on all of life. This includes sermons that have the needs of the people in mind. If our sermons are nothing but correction or rebuke, they may be

---

8. Cosper, *Rhythms of Grace*, 124.

true but can easily lead to abuse and manipulation. If they are nothing but encouragement, they can lead to excusing sin or inciting indifference toward holiness. The regular preaching of God's Word considers what people need to hear and how they need to hear it. The best preachers know the people in front of them and apply the timeless truth of God's Word to timely situations in our world.

Another feature of the sermon related to corporate formation is the need to promote sound doctrine. Corporate formation includes preaching that is faithful to the gospel and core doctrines of the Christian faith. A sermon can exposit the Scriptures and never touch on the gospel or emphasize core doctrines. This means that all preaching, whether in Proverbs or in Philippians, needs to highlight the gospel message. We don't need to perform interpretative gymnastics to focus upon the redemptive work of Jesus Christ as the main message of Scripture. Julius Kim states: "One of the most compelling reasons preachers should interpret and preach Christ from all the Scriptures is because Jesus and the apostles did it. Jesus and his disciples interpreted the Scriptures—which for them was the Hebrew Bible (the Old Testament)—in light of the person and work of Jesus Christ, the Messiah-King."[9] The arc of Scripture bends toward the person and work of Jesus Christ. If a Jewish or Muslim person could hear a sermon and find it agreeable, then we're doing it wrong. Sermons must also keep Christian doctrinal categories in mind. We don't jettison

---

9. Julius J. Kim, *Preaching the Whole Counsel of God's Word: Design and Deliver Gospel-Centered Sermons* (Grand Rapids, MI: Zondervan, 2015), 52.

theology in preaching. We must recognize that Scripture and theology are partners. Sound doctrine arises from and is confirmed by the Scriptures. Any sermon that disputes or disposes of sound doctrine should be held in suspicion. Faithful preaching of the text maintains, rather than disdains, Christian doctrine.

When it comes to the application of the text, preaching with corporate formation in mind includes connecting the text to the mission of God and the ministry of the church. While applications are diverse, they almost always fall under the umbrella of the mission and ministry of the church. While it ultimately depends on the Holy Spirit to take the Word of God and apply it to the people of God, the instrument by which that often takes place is the sermon. God calls pastors to both correctly teach the Word *and* shepherd the flock among them (2 Tim. 2:15; 1 Pet. 5:2). This means that the best shepherds teach correctly for the sake of calling their people to action and service. If the encouragement is to rest in the promises of God in Christ, leaders may encourage us to make those promises known to others. If the call is to serve in the church, leaders might highlight the needs of our church community. If the call is to be more faithful in personal or family discipleship, leaders could provide resources and avenues for helping God's people in those areas. In this way, pastors drive God's Word into the hearts and onto the hands of their people, trusting the Spirit to move and complete the work.

Essential Means 4: The Word through Sacrament

Before proceeding, let me explain my use of the word *sacrament*. This is a loaded term and contains a lot of baggage for Protestant evangelicals. The idea of sacrament would seem to indicate a desire to move toward Roman Catholicism or Eastern Orthodoxy. May it never be! I certainly do not want to present a stumbling block to you. If so, the word *ordinance* is just as sound and faithful to Scripture. But the reason why I want to consider rescuing the word *sacrament* is because it is intended to describe the profound truth of God's grace communicated through specific events and acts within the church. Historically, Protestants have been comfortable with the word *sacrament* so long as it did not equate to earning salvation, and so long as it was limited to two specific acts empowered by the words of Christ: baptism and the Lord's Supper. Church historian Michael Haykin has shown that, specifically for Baptists in the past, the notion of viewing baptism and Communion as sacraments was normal.[10] To view baptism and the Lord's Supper in this way is simply to demonstrate their deep spiritual significance and their intimate connection to our union with Christ. Corporate formation is defined by baptism and the Supper; there is no corporate spiritual formation without them.

The church of my youth was committed to the weekly observance of the Lord's Supper. My father was integral in the facilitation of the Lord's Supper on Sunday mornings. I

10. See Michael A. G. Haykin, *Amidst Us Our Belovèd Stands: Recovering Sacrament in the Baptist Tradition* (Bellingham, WA: Lexham Press, 2022).

remember arriving early to church with my dad to prepare tray after tray of juice-filled cups and broken wafers. My favorite part was using the white Communion cup–filling dispenser (which probably resulted in many stained church clothes). Placing the trays through the worship center, my father would then proceed to find volunteers to serve the Lord's Supper. It was a thoroughly lay-led endeavor and, in many ways, displayed the beauty of the local church in its simple, yet profound, work of worshiping the Lord. I came to greatly appreciate the work required in making sure the Lord's Supper was prepared and distributed every Sunday. I didn't know there was any other way until I found myself convictionally in a different theological tradition later in life. Apparently, there were Christians who didn't celebrate the Supper on a weekly basis! This seemed strange and unnatural to me. And although I feel like the Lord's Supper was more mechanical than meaningful in my earlier church experience, I have never lost the conviction that the Supper is pivotal to Christian spirituality and best practiced in a weekly manner.

Corporate formation means taking the practice of the Lord's Supper seriously. Paul's admonishment and instructions regarding the Lord's Supper in 1 Corinthians 11:17–32 assumes a regular weekly practice of the Supper. Biblical scholar Gordon Fee notes: "The Corinthian problem was not their failure to gather, but their failure truly to be God's new people when they gathered."[11] Gathering was not the issue,

---

[11] Gordon D. Fee, *The First Epistle to the Corinthians*, The New International Commentary on the New Testament (Grand Rapids, MI: Wm. B. Eerdmans Publishing, 1987), 536.

but gathering with the right heart and focus was. Divisions had arisen in the church, making the spirit and purpose of the Lord's Supper all but void. The Supper is intended to be a symbol of our unity, not a reason for division. The Supper is one of the defining marks of our unity in Christ where there is no longer the identity of "Jew or Greek, slave or free, [or] male and female" (Gal. 3:28). The Supper is the means of grace by which we remember the incarnation of Christ, the atonement of Christ, the resurrection of Christ, and the future return of Christ. Indeed, Paul states: "For as often as you eat this bread and drink the cup, you proclaim the Lord's death until he comes" (1 Cor. 11:26). The Supper is a sign of hope, love, mercy, and grace, communicating that our greatest need has been accomplished by the Son who took on flesh for our sake. It is a recognition that Christ dwells with his people by his Spirit. We are reminded of our bond with each other and our union with Christ, and we neglect the Supper to our detriment.

The sacrament or ordinance of baptism is even more foundational. Entrance to the table of the Christ presumes a baptism into the life of Christ. It is the mark of Christian discipleship. It is the entrance into the life of the triune God and the life of the church. It is a symbol of our regeneration, our new birth in Christ, and should be undertaken with the utmost sincerity. Baptism is *the* life commitment of a new believer in Christ, one who has understood the work of Christ on their behalf, and publicly chooses to identify with Christ through baptism. Whereas the old covenant was marked with circumcision based on ethnic affiliation with the Jewish people, the new covenant is marked with baptism based on spiritual affiliation with Christ. He is the promised seed and the one who fulfills all the promises of God (see Gal. 3:16; 2 Cor. 1:20). There has always been one family of God, but with the new covenant in Christ, we now enter that family through baptism. The old covenant was based on physical birth; the new covenant is based on spiritual rebirth. Whether someone is six or sixty, their baptism is and should be a significant part of their spiritual journey.

Baptism and the Lord's Supper are essential means of grace for corporate formation, which in turn impacts our personal formation. Both sacraments point to the abiding presence of Christ in the church and his members. We are reborn in Christ "by grace through faith" (Eph. 2:8), called to put off our old self and put on the new self in Christ (see Eph. 4:22–24). Christians should hold baptism in high regard, and subsequently, we need to practice the Lord's Supper as it acknowledges the presence and work of Christ among us. Baptism and the Lord's Supper bring us together to proclaim the gospel and continually sanctify us as we worship him together.

Essential Means 5: The Word through Service

Jesus made clear that his kingdom is not like what we experience in the world, where power and position are important, but "the Son of Man did not come to be served, but to serve" (Matt. 20:28). When we have an attitude of service, we inhabit the posture and character of Christ. Christ's love transforms us to serve and love others. Corporate formation recognizes that the love of Christ is the foundation of service (see Gal. 5:13). A heart of service also leads the church to identify and cultivate the gifts of its people. Peter tells the church: "Just as each one has received a gift, use it to serve others, as good stewards of the varied grace of God" (1 Pet. 4:10). Our gifts are a sign of God's grace and are used to share that grace of God with others. When people are encouraged to use the gifts that God has given them in the local church, marvelous things happen.

Serving is something every Christ-follower is called to do; the question is where and how. When it comes to gifts in the local church, it's tempting for us to highlight and prioritize the more public gifts. When I worked in small group ministry, I made it my mission to ensure all group leaders remembered this one thing: be normal. Be the person that God has made you to be. It is amazing how many of us think that we are inadequate for the Kingdom simply because we don't have the gifts and skills of the person on stage. Too many of us feel deficient or unusable simply because we have not been encouraged to see our gifts as vital and necessary for God's kingdom. The Holy Spirit thinks otherwise. Paul explains: "The eye cannot say to the hand, 'I don't need you!' Or again, the head can't say to the feet, 'I don't need you!' On the contrary, those parts of the body that are weaker are indispensable" (1 Cor. 12:21–22). We

> When people are encouraged to use the gifts that God has given them in the local church, marvelous things happen.

need each other to function as the complete body of Christ. The church fails when we prioritize one gift to the neglect of the others.

A dedication to corporate formation means everyone is called to serve regardless of position. We should never tire of hearing Paul's exhortation: "Do nothing out of selfish ambition or conceit, but in humility consider others as more important than yourselves" (Phil. 2:3). Whether or not your name is on the church sign, you are called to a life of service to others. Certainly, there is a place to understand the role of the shepherd and their necessary duties, but when ministry leaders let this temptation take hold it leads to pride and contempt. Leaders lead by serving. They model through humility. Leadership positions do not exempt one from serving. If anything, it increases one's responsibility to serve and lead others to do so. The best leaders equip others to serve and help them see their contribution as valuable for God's kingdom and the good of others. A serving church, with serving leaders, is a church filled with grace that spills out into their everyday lives.

> **The best leaders equip others to serve and help them see their contribution as valuable for God's kingdom and the good of others.**

Essential Means 6: The Word through Sacrifice

Dallas Willard observed: "Strangely enough, even though sacrifice may seem more of a service, it is always more of a discipline. Our need to give is greater than God's need to receive, because he is always well supplied. But how nourishing to our faith are the tokens of God's care in response to our sacrifice."[12] In sacrificial living, we experience the sustaining grace of God in fresh and exciting ways. Corporately we need to be attuned to the needs of others to the point that we can and will sacrifice as needed for the good of the other. In fact, corporate spiritual formation provides us space to be humble and giving. Paul encourages the church to submit to one another out of fear and reverence for Christ (Eph. 5:21). For those who have experienced the work of Christ in their lives, empowered by the Spirit, we understand that losing our lives is gaining it. We pour ourselves out for the sake of others. Whether a one-time act or a prolonged season, the spirit of sacrifice remains. Corporate formation recognizes that through sacrificial living for the sake of others, we walk in the very footsteps of Christ who calls us to follow him by denying ourselves and taking up our cross daily (see Luke 9:23).

Corporate spiritual formation also recognizes that without the community, we have little context to live sacrificially. Paul's analogy of the body in 1 Corinthians 12 is helpful to understand just how much we need each other. When a part of the body is injured or faltering, we need the other parts to step in. Paul exhorts the church: "Carry one another's burdens; in this way you will fulfill the law of Christ" (Gal. 6:2). The law of Christ is the law of love and sacrificial living. Timothy George states: "We all have burdens, and God does not intend

---

12. Dallas Willard, *The Spirit of the Disciplines: Understanding How God Changes Lives* (New York, NY: HarperCollins, 1988), 175.

for us to carry them by ourselves in isolation from our brothers and sisters. . . . The myth of self-sufficiency is not a mark of bravery but rather a sign of pride."[13] We are called into a "burden-bearing" life in the church. Not everyone is called to do the exact same thing, as Paul elaborates in Galatians 6, but collectively we carry each other's burdens. This desire to fulfill the law of Christ makes us more generous with our time and resources. When we commit to live sacrificially, we put ourselves in the pathway to experience the grace and provision of God.

Essential Means 7: The Word through Study

Studies continue to show Americans are unfamiliar with the Bible, if they even engage it at all.[14] Regarding biblical illiteracy, Trevin Wax notes: "Many Americans know next to nothing about the Bible. And, for those who do have rudimentary understanding of certain Bible stories and facts, it is likely they picked up their knowledge about the Bible from someone else, not from the scriptural text itself."[15] Surveys show

---

13. Timothy George, *Galatians*, The New American Commentary, vol. 30 (Nashville, TN: B&H Publishers, 1994), 413–14.

14. For a recent study by Lifeway Research see Bob Smietana, "Lifeway Research: Americans Are Fond of the Bible, Don't Actually Read It," Lifeway Research, April 25, 2017, https://research.lifeway.com/2017/04/25/lifeway-research-americans-are-fond-of-the-bible-dont-actually-read-it/.

15. Trevin Wax, "Pastors, the Bible Is the Best Thing You've Got Going," The Gospel Coalition, May 2, 2022, https://www.thegospelcoalition.org/blogs/trevin-wax/pastors-the-bible-is-the-best-thing-youve-got-going/.

that Americans still have a generally positive view of the Bible, they simply don't know what it's about. Churchgoers fare a little better on this, but that's only assuming they are hearing solid expository preaching. Regardless, there is always a need for increased biblical literacy among Christians. Jen Wilkin hits the biblical literacy nail right on the head: "Both the false teacher and the secular humanist rely on biblical ignorance for their messages to take root, and the modern church has proven fertile ground for those messages. Because we do not know our Bibles, we crumble at the most basic challenges to our worldview."[16] Nothing can replace a direct engagement with God's Word.

Corporate study allows certain members of the body of Christ to exercise their gifts, as well as brings Christ's people together to bring new insight. Maybe you've been in a group where a leader goes around and asks a question like, "And what does this text mean to you?" That's not what I'm after here. Corporate Bible study takes seriously the proper interpretation of Scripture, but it also takes to heart that we can work together to bring great insight out of the biblical text. Not only that, but we can also share how God's timeless and trustworthy Word has impacted specific parts of our life. We can grow in our knowledge of how to care and pray for one another. We also collectively grow in our appreciation for the immeasurable riches contained in God's Word. Together we can proclaim with the psalmist: "I delight in your commands,

---

16. Jen Wilkin, *Women of the Word: How to Study the Bible with Both Our Hearts and Our Minds* (Wheaton, IL: Crossway, 2014), 47.

which I love. I will lift up my hands to your commands, which I love, and will meditate on your statutes" (Ps. 119:47–48).

Group study, whether in a Sunday school or weekly study outside of Sunday morning, provides a more in-depth opportunity to devote oneself to the apostles' teaching. While a biblically sound and doctrinally astute sermon is key (see Essential Means 1), we need environments to explore God's Word and sound doctrine in more detail. Being trained in sound doctrine is an ongoing and multivarious task. To equip saints for biblical literacy, specific structures should be in place to ensure these tasks are accomplished. It's not a question of *if* Christians need to study God's Word, but *how*. Christian formation demands that we take equipping the saints to understand God's Word seriously. The study of God's Word is a means of grace because it leads us closer to the God of grace and love. If study leads us to love anything more than God, then we are doing it wrong. Jen Wilkin says it well: "Our study of the Bible is only beneficial insofar as it increases our love for the God it proclaims. Bible study is a means to an end, not an end in and of itself. It is a means to love God more, and to live differently because we have learned to behold him better. And it is a means to become what we behold."[17]

> **Christian formation demands that we take equipping the saints to understand God's Word seriously.**

---

17. Wilkin, *Women of the Word*, 158.

Final Thoughts

The local church is indispensable to Christian spiritual formation. It might be true, however, that your church has a long way to go for healthy spiritual formation to take place. It may also be true that you have stepped away from the church for any number of reasons. For many, the church has not been a safe place. If that is the case for you, I am deeply sorry and I pray that the Lord would provide a space for healing with people who will minister compassionate and Christlike care for your soul. The church is meant to be a place of nurture and love, not fear and hate. We will all experience wounds and hurts from time to time, even in the healthiest local church. We have a perfect Savior who is perfecting his people by his Spirit through the work of his imperfect church. Only in glory will we see the fullness of what God

> The church is meant to be a place of nurture and love, not fear and hate.

is doing through us and in the church. So don't give up on the church entirely! Though you may require a long season of healing, I hope that part of that healing can take place in a thriving and godly community of saints who are dedicated to one another and your spiritual formation.

So how do we experience and grow in the grace of God? Go to church. Fellowship with the saints is the primary way to grow in our relationship with Jesus Christ and one another. It is worship and gathering with the saints that nurtures our formation; therefore, Christians since the beginning of the church have gathered to hear the Word of God read and preached, to pray for one another, and to break bread and experience the presence of Christ together. The essence of Christian worship is hearing the Word read, having teaching that explains the Scriptures, singing songs of joy and sorrow, tasting the Lord's Supper, welcoming new believers through baptism, and coming together to encourage one another. The writer of Hebrews gives us this encouragement: "Let us hold on to the confession of our hope without wavering, since he who promised is faithful. And let us consider one another in order to provoke love and good works, not neglecting to gather together, as some are in the habit of doing, but encouraging each other, and all the more as you see the day approaching" (Heb. 10:23–25). If you truly wish to experience Christian spiritual formation, you *must* be involved in the body of Christ. Individualism is a sign of our pride and arrogance, not spiritual growth. One must be in the body of Christ to truly experience the grace of God and to grow into the image of Christ.

Resources for Further Study

Gregg R. Allison. *The Church: An Introduction*. Wheaton, IL: Crossway, 2021.

Dustin Benge. *The Loveliest Place: The Beauty and Glory of the Church*. Wheaton, IL: Crossway, 2022.

Mark Dever. *The Church: The Gospel Made Visible*. Nashville, TN: B&H Academic, 2012.

Collin Hansen and Jonathan Leeman. *Rediscover Church: Why the Body of Christ Is Essential.* Wheaton, IL: Crossway, 2021.

James Wilhoit. *Spiritual Formation as if the Church Mattered: Growing in Christ through Community.* Rev. ed. Grand Rapids, MI: Baker Academic, 2022.

Questions for Reflection

1. What has been your experience of formation in the local church? Take a moment to write down the different activities of your context that you consider pivotal to your spiritual formation.

2. In what ways do you see the Word of Christ dwelling richly among your local church (see Col. 3:16)? In what ways is it lacking?

3. Would you consider your practice of the Lord's Supper and baptism to be consistent with the descriptions given in this chapter? Would you say their practice is seen as pivotal to discipleship or tangential in your church?

4. How is the study of God's Word accomplished in your local church? If not emphasized, what steps could you take to emphasize the study of God's Word in community?

5. Do you see the local church as a hindrance or help in formation? If you have been hurt by the local church, take a moment

to journal through those thoughts. Share those with someone you trust and ask how you might be able to seek growth and reconciliation if necessary.

CHAPTER 6

Formation of the Personal Body

How happy is the one who does not walk in the advice
of the wicked or stand in the pathway with sinners or sit
in the company of mockers! Instead, his delight is in the
LORD's instruction, and he meditates on it day and night.
—PSALM 1:1–2

By means of the Disciplines, let the truths of the gospel
restore your soul.
—DONALD WHITNEY[1]

I hope by now I have convinced you that there is no replace-
ment for corporate spiritual formation. The church, as
Colin Hansen and Jonathan Leeman note, "forms us into men
and women of God . . . [where] we learn more about who

---

1. Donald S. Whitney, *Spiritual Disciplines for the Christian Life*,
revised and updated (Colorado Springs, CO: NavPress, 2014), 20.

God intended us to be as individuals—our unique abilities and passions."[2] In community with others, we discover more about who we are and how we are wired. Corporate formation does not mold us into Jesus robots, it emphasizes the unique makeup of one body with many members. What we do in the body of Christ affects each member, for better or worse. This is why corporate formation is so foundational, yet often neglected. I cannot stress enough the need for healthy corporate formation as foundational for healthy personal formation.

I hope to present both the "why" of personal spiritual formation as well as several "hows." This is what Christian spiritual formation is all about: beholding the beauty of God. God calls us out by his goodness, to be shaped by his truth, to enjoy and behold his beauty. This process is lifelong, which means we should not expect instantaneous growth (as discussed in chapter 4). Thus, personal formation requires perseverance, walking in step with the Spirit and continually leaning upon the finished work of Christ. Personal formation also looks different for everybody. While we can learn from others, imitating their own walk with Christ, we must remember that the Spirit is working in and through each of us differently. When we begin

> **God calls us out by his goodness, to be shaped by his truth, to enjoy and behold his beauty.**

2. Colin Hansen and Jonathan Leeman, *Rediscover Church: Why the Body of Christ is Essential* (Wheaton, IL: Crossway, 2021), 144.

comparing our spiritual growth to others, we can easily become discouraged and lose sight of what God is doing through us.

Slaying the Personal Formation Boogeyman

Before going any further, there is a formation "boogeyman" that needs to be dealt with. You might recall earlier how I mentioned the idea of Gnosticism, the ancient belief that matter is evil and salvation is related to special knowledge. While church leaders in the first few centuries dealt a big blow against Gnostic teaching, the ghost of Gnosticism continues to haunt evangelical churches. We see this particularly when it comes to spiritual formation.

First, we are prone to want the "magic formula" or "seven secrets" to unlock our spiritual life. Some so-called Christian teachers may even promise you results if you just follow their teaching/read their book/join their church/give money to their ministry/etc. This is exactly what Gnostics in the first centuries promised: special knowledge that they alone possessed. Some even said they learned it directly from Jesus himself. Don't be fooled. There is no secret to personal spiritual formation, only a commitment to follow Christ and be led by his Word.

Second, we are prone to believe that our physicality has little to do with formation. In other words, what we do with our bodies has little bearing upon our spirituality. Ring, ring, Gnosticism is calling. When we separate what we do with our bodies from our spiritual life, we may be engaging in spiritual formation, but it's not *Christian* spiritual formation. Christian doctrine declares that our bodies matter. If you need proof, look to the incarnation of Christ. Yes, our bodies are subject to sin and the Fall, but they are no less valuable. We are looking toward bodily redemption, not bodily destruction. Paul says that "we also groan within ourselves, eagerly waiting for adoption, the redemption of our bodies" (Rom. 8:23). So, when considering personal formation, remember that the body matters. We'll get more into this shortly.

The final aspect of the spiritual formation boogeyman we must slay is something we covered in chapter 4 but bears repeating: personal disciplines do *not* save you. The person and work of Christ is the basis of our salvation. No amount of Bible memorization or prayer times can contribute to your salvation. Christ has accomplished it all. For those who have trusted in Christ, we have been given a new life and new desires. Out of that new life and new heart, we pursue holiness and the things of God through personal discipline. While personal discipline may clarify your salvation, it does not establish it.

So having slayed the formation boogeyman, we need to be careful lest he be resurrected. When it comes to the pursuit of personal spiritual formation, our fallen hearts are prone to fall into old habits, old ways of thinking, and most of all, into selfish pride. If you see the hand of the boogeyman reaching out of the grave, pray for the Lord to give you humility and to refresh your heart with the truth of the gospel.

The Spirituality of the Word

I have always been an advocate for simplicity. Just ask my wife. Every so often I'll go through a period of wanting to get rid of old (yet still perfectly good!) clothes and home items for the sake of simplifying our life. If I haven't worn it or used it in the last twelve months, it's a prime candidate for the donation bin. I try to think the same way with technology. Though I still have a smartphone, I have tried to make it look and feel as "dumb" as possible. When shopping for new clothes, I have a certain brand and type of shoes/shirts/jeans/etc. that I like, and I rarely deviate from those brands. I've always tried to live by a "less is more" mentality. Though I'm not a full-on minimalist, I closely identify with the sentiment. This probably has influenced my spiritual life in various ways as well, though I tend to think it has made a positive impact. So, indulge me as I present a "less is more" approach to personal spiritual formation.

I believe spiritual disciplines boil down to one simple thing: saturating our lives with the Word of God. Specifically, I think we will never go wrong if we emphasize the intake of God's Word and its impact on our prayer lives as the fundamentals of Christian spirituality. If we choose to focus on reading, studying, memorizing, and using Scripture in our everyday lives, we will never go wrong in the spiritual life. Similarly, if we view our intake of God's Word as fuel for our prayer lives, we will see beautiful things happen. Let me explain what I mean by the "spirituality of the Word"

> I believe spiritual disciplines boil down to one simple thing: saturating our lives with the Word of God.

and then move toward specific ways the Word can better infiltrate our hearts and minds.

Everything in our personal spirituality is grounded upon
God's Word. Our personal spiritual formation is only effective
insofar as it is guided by Scripture. This does not mean that
we must have an open Bible everywhere we go, but it means
that the sufficiency and authority of Scripture is our best bet
for spiritual growth. The Spirit uses a conversation, a text
message, a song, or several other things to further our sanctification. But that song or text brings growth only if it's connected in some way to the truth of God's Word. So we're back
to where we started—the Scriptures. The Word of God is primary in our formation because it informs all other areas of our
spiritual life. Simply put: apart from the Word, there is no
means of grace. We are to be like the psalmist who declares: "I
will never forget your precepts,
for you have given me life
through them" (Ps. 119:93). We
should affirm with Paul that not
only is all Scripture inspired by
God, but it is "profitable for
teaching, for rebuking, for cor-
recting, for training in righteousness, so that the man of
God may be complete, equipped for every good work" (2 Tim.
3:16–17). We are not only commanded to prioritize God's
Word, but we need to remember that only God's Word brings
the most joy and satisfaction. A spirituality that is shaped by
anything less than Scripture is not Christian.

> **A spirituality
> that is shaped
> by anything less
> than Scripture is
> not Christian.**

A Life of Bible Intake

I still have the first Bible my parents gave me at my baptism. It's a brown leather NIV with a gold lettering inscription on the front cover. I recently took it back up as a reading Bible for a season. It was fun to see what junior high and high school Coleman highlighted, underlined, and wrote in the margins. Apparently, something was getting through! Though I don't remember exactly when and how much I was reading the Bible back then, it seems that some sort of Bible intake was happening. When it comes to a life of Bible intake, David Mathis says, "[We] come away from our Bible intake with a more satisfied soul, which imparts a flavor and demeanor to our lives and decision-making that affects everything."[3] Don Whitney makes a similar observation: "No Spiritual Discipline is more important than the intake of God's Word. Nothing can substitute for it. There simply is no healthy Christian life apart from a diet of the milk and meat of Scripture."[4] Our joy in God is directly related to our journey in Scripture. The more we explore the Bible, the more it leads us to the beauty of God and his plan of redemption. Thus, we need Bible intake like we need oxygen. Without it, our Christian formation suffocates and eventually dies.

There are numerous ways that Bible intake occurs. For many people, we encounter the Bible first through hearing it in some form or fashion. Even non-Christians have likely heard various snippets of Scripture (though, probably out of

---

3. David Mathis, *Habits of Grace: Enjoying Jesus Through the Spiritual Disciplines* (Wheaton, IL: Crossway, 2016), 64.
4. Whitney, *Spiritual Disciplines for the Christian Life*, 22.

context). Paul says, "So faith comes from what is heard, and what is heard comes through the message about Christ" (Rom. 10:17). Listening to God's Word, whether in church or in the car, is a great way to take in God's Word.[5] Most Bible apps for smartphones have an audio version. Some apps such as Dwell are specifically designed to listen to the Bible in various translations, with different voices, and even with different background music!

> The more we explore the Bible, the more it leads us to the beauty of God and his plan of redemption. Thus, we need Bible intake like we need oxygen. Without it, our Christian formation suffocates and eventually dies.

The next way for Bible intake is reading God's Word. Personal Bible reading is foundational to personal spiritual formation. Sounds easy, right? Well, there is a reason this is called a *discipline*; we must discipline ourselves to prioritize reading God's Word. Don Whitney provides three essential elements for Bible reading: find time, find a plan, and meditate.[6] We'll get to meditation in a moment, but I have found Whitney's prescription to be

---

5. For those who are physically unable to hear, I hope you get great joy from "hearing" the Word of God here: https://www.deafmissions.com/aslv2020/.

6. Whitney, *Spiritual Disciplines for the Christian Life*, 28–30.

exactly right. For time, you may need to rearrange some things in your day to prioritize reading. Getting up a few minutes earlier can have significant spiritual payoff. Taking ten minutes during a lunch break can fill your spiritual tank more than whatever you just ate. I personally do a variation of Bible plans. On my audio Bible app, I do a five-days-a-week plan since I'm commuting in the car about five days a week. At home, usually in the mornings, I use the M'Cheyne reading plan. In between, whether during a break in the day or at night, I try to read five chapters from Psalms and one chapter from Proverbs, which means I will read through each of these books once a month if I'm consistent. Your life rhythm may be different, so adjust accordingly. Are there days when I neglect my Bible reading plan? Absolutely. The beauty of the plan is that you just pick up where you left off. If having dates like "May 4" or "June 21" trips you up in a reading plan, forget those dates are even there. Who cares if you are reading for December 11 when it's January 30? The point is you are working through a plan for the purpose of reading God's Word.

Reading God's Word should lead us to the study and memorization of God's Word. While I believe study is a corporate endeavor, Bible study must include the personal task of working through a text for the sake of greater understanding. When it comes to Bible study, Jen Wilkin contends: "We must learn to study in such a way that we are not just absorbing the insights of another, but are actually being equipped to interpret and apply Scripture on our own."[7] Coupled with a

---

7. Jen Wilkin, *Women of the Word: How to Study the Bible with Both Our Hearts and Our Minds* (Wheaton, IL: Crossway, 2014), 47.

dedicated group study, personal study of God's Word brings the Scriptures to life in fresh and exciting ways. The story of redemption, biblical doctrine, and historical backgrounds to the Bible all come together to help you better appreciate and understand what God's Word is about.

While reading and studying, we should seek to memorize Scripture as well. Admittedly, this is the area where I'm weakest. I'm good at working through a plan, but I often do not take the time to stop and memorize portions of Scripture that I'm reading. I have a pretty good recall of Scripture, and some texts I've memorized through repeated reading, but I often neglect to memorize as a discipline. Memorizing God's Word is vital for numerous reasons. Memorization provides an opportunity to recall Scripture when sharing the gospel or encouraging a fellow believer. When we have Scripture stored up in our hearts, we can more ably fight sin and encourage our own weary heart with God's truth.

The next way that we can bring Scripture into our hearts and minds is through meditation. Perhaps you associate that word with eastern mysticism or New Age spirituality, but I assure you that the term and the practice is biblical and foundational for our spiritual formation. Let me explain. Biblical meditation is the concentrated effort to take a verse or portion of Scripture and a prolonged time considering the meaning, its content, and otherwise focusing intently upon all that it has to say. The Puritan Thomas Watson argued: "The reason we come away so cold from reading the word is, because we

do not warm ourselves at the fire of meditation."[8] Meditating
on the Word of God brings us ever closer to the heart of God.
It drives the nail of God's love further into our hearts. Unlike
worldly meditation which asks you to free your mind, biblical meditation fills our minds with the truth of God. It is
active, not passive. It also leads us to act and pray more read-
ily. When we meditate upon God's Word we are "like a tree
planted beside flowing streams that bears its fruit in its season, and its leaf does not wither. Whatever [we do] prospers"
(Ps. 1:3). When we are connected to the flowing streams of
the Spirit through biblical meditation, we are sure to remain
firmly planted in the Lord.

A Life of Prayer

I believe when we prioritize Scripture in our lives, it can't
help but affect our prayer life. The study, memorization, and
meditation upon God's Word fills our hearts and gushes forth
in prayer. We should also see the Bible as the very words we
can use to pray back to God. Don Whitney makes this case in
his book *Praying the Bible*. Rather than saying the same old
things about the same old things, take a passage of Scripture
and pray through it, allowing the Spirit to recall specific people and situations prompted by the very text you are reading.[9]

---

8. Thomas Watson, "How We May Read the Scriptures with Most
Spiritual Profit" in James Nichols, ed. *Puritan Sermons 1659–1689 in
Six Volumes*, vol. 2 (Wheaton, IL: Richard Owen Roberts, Publishers,
1981), 62.

9. For more on this, see Donald S. Whitney, *Praying the Bible*
(Wheaton, IL: Crossway, 2015).

This is the perfect way to ensure that a spirituality of the Word infiltrates every facet of your spiritual life. So if you are stuck in a rut with your prayer life, pick up your Bible, take your reading plan, and get to praying. If the text speaks to God's faithfulness, ask that God would help a friend who seems to be wandering from the faith. If the text speaks to the life of Christ, ask the Spirit to recall a family member or friend who doesn't yet know Jesus. If the text speaks to suffering, ask God to bring comfort to a church member who is battling cancer. And so on. Let the text guide your prayer life as you read the text. Your Bible reading and your prayer life can work together to uncover greater depths of spiritual treasures.

> "We find complete silence shocking because it leaves the impression that nothing is happening. In a go-go world such as ours, what could be worse than that!"
> —Dallas Willard[10]

Starting with the Word as the foundation for prayer, I want to briefly encourage you to take the next step in your life of prayer. Silence and solitude amplify prayer and magnify God's Word. Silence and solitude give us opportunities to put our soul before God, free from distraction. We also learn the value of silence and solitude from Jesus himself. Following the beheading of John the Baptist, Jesus withdrew "to a remote

10. Dallas Willard, *The Spirit of the Disciplines: Understanding How God Changes Lives* (New York, NY: HarperOne, 1990), 163.

place to be alone" (Matt. 14:13). At other times, Jesus "went out to the mountain to pray and spent all night in prayer to God" (Luke 6:12). Jesus knew the value and necessity of retreating alone to pray. Though Jesus set the example, our world today creates an even greater need for silence and solitude for the purpose of prayer. In a culture which is filled with noise and busyness, the most countercultural thing we can do is seek silence and solitude. Don Whitney says, "Without silence and solitude we can be active, but shallow. Without fellowship we can be deep, but stagnant. Christlikeness requires both sides of the equation."[11] It's important to remember that silence and solitude are two sides of the same spiritual coin. They provide a unique space and opportunity to seek God through prayer or Scripture reading. In silence, we temporarily abstain from speaking to concentrate on speaking to God

> Silence and solitude amplify prayer and magnify God's Word. Silence and solitude give us opportunities to put our soul before God, free from distraction.

from our heart. Solitude includes a temporary withdrawal or retreat. We can choose to take time to be silent while sitting in the car, in the office, or at home. When we seek solitude it's not to be away from others primarily, but to be with the Lord. It's perfectly healthy to desire and have alone time.

---

11. Whitney, *Spiritual Disciplines for the Christian Life*, 225.

Solitude is a purposeful posture to hear God. To practice silence and solitude, we need to slow down and be purposeful with our time. This requires creating margin in one's life—which is certainly easier said than done, depending on the season of your life. With three kids, it seems that the word *margin* is a foreign language in our home. I need to be sensitive to my wife, asking her when and how she wants to have space for spiritual growth. If married, you need to have this category in mind. If single, you need to ensure that other things don't crowd in and remove purposeful time of silence and solitude. Whether young or old, married or single, we all need to be attentive to the need for silence and solitude for the sake of engaging God in prayer.

Every Christian would benefit from more silence and solitude in their life, but ministry leaders, especially, need to carve out space for silence and solitude. I feel like one of the most neglected disciplines for ministers is prayer in silence and solitude. You may not think this is the case, but ministry schedules, hospital visits, sermon preparation, pastoral counseling, and more make the need for silence and solitude vital for ministry health. Doing work for God must be fueled by solitude with God. If the Son of God understood the need for this, so should church leaders today. Budget short moments throughout the week for silence and solitude, as well as a larger amount on a monthly or

> **Fill your time with more silence and solitude than strategic planning.**

quarterly basis. I recommend that churches with the resources for multiday staff retreats fill your time with more silence and solitude than strategic planning. As the spiritual health of a minister increases, so, too, does the health of the ministry and church. This leads me to the last spiritual discipline I want to emphasize. Connected to a spirituality of the Word and a life of prayer is a dedication to regular biblical fasting.

A Life of Fasting

Fasting is the one spiritual discipline we are more prone to talk about than practice. You may have practiced something like intermittent fasting to lose weight. This may be valuable as a lifestyle choice, but this is not what I mean when I talk about fasting. Biblical fasting has a specific spiritual goal in mind. Any health benefits are secondary to the intended goal of intentionally seeking to create a greater hunger for God. Fasting, like silence and solitude, is countercultural because it is the decision to deny yourself food or another object for the sake of something greater than yourself. The goal of fasting is always more of God. We may fast to seek God's wisdom, to dedicate a special time of prayer and Scripture reading, to express grief and lament, or all the above. Christians fast, as Jesus modeled, to show that we do not "live on bread alone but on every word that comes from the mouth of God" (Matt. 4:4). We do not fast to test our own will but to submit ourselves to God's will. John Piper, in his book *Hunger for God*, states: "God rewards fasting because fasting expresses the cry of the heart that nothing on the earth can satisfy our souls besides God."[12] Fasting is a means of grace because it helps us see and rely upon God more than ourselves and material goods. Whether we are fasting from food or phones, the goal is to give up ourselves to gain God.

Don Whitney says it well when he observes: "Christians in a gluttonous, denial-less, self-indulgent society may struggle to accept and to begin the practice of fasting. Few Disciplines go so radically against the flesh and the mainstream of culture as this one."[13] Fasting is not meant to showcase our strength, but God's. Jesus denounced the Pharisees for making a big show out of their fasting; godly fasting is best done in secret (see Matt. 6:16–18). This does not mean no one should ever know about your fast, but the point is that fasting is meant to be focused on making much of God, not ourselves. Whether it's a fast from one meal or an entire day of eating, we do so to humble ourselves before God as an act of worship.

If fasting has not been a regular part of your spiritual life, let me encourage you to start small. Seek guidance from a trusted friend and perhaps a doctor, depending on your health situation. Also remember that we don't stumble into a fast. Forgetting to eat lunch does not count. Fasting is a conscious decision, planned and executed with a particular spiritual focus in mind. Even if we are fasting from an activity like watching TV or using our smartphone, we must plan out our commitment and even write down some goals beforehand. If fasting from a meal or multiple meals, we may need to prepare

---

12. John Piper, *Hunger for God: Desiring God through Fasting and Prayer*, rev. ed. (Wheaton, IL: Crossway, 2013), 162.

13. Whitney, *Spiritual Disciplines for the Christian Life*, 191.

physically by resting well and eating appropriately beforehand. Though this is a personal discipline, it may help to have a partner or commit as a small group to a fast for accountability. Also, prepare for opposition and spiritual warfare. Satan does not want God's people engaging in fasting for spiritual growth. At the same time, do not give into condemnation if the fast does not go as planned. Make another plan to try again. The point is to pursue a greater hunger for God. One step at a time is okay. While spiritual insight may come during the fast, it might not be until long after that you see the fruit of your concentrated time with the Lord. I would also consider journaling before, during, and after your experience. Remember that God answers the prayers of the humble (see James 4:6), but he may not always do so right away. Last, as with Bible intake and prayer, your fasting is most effective when connected to the Word. Fasting itself is a biblical discipline, but it's best seen as a means to greater prayer and meditation upon Scripture.

A Rule of Life

The final encouragement I want to provide is to consider creating what has been traditionally called a "rule of life." This is nothing more than a purposeful ordering of your life to prioritize spiritual activity. Another way to describe this might be your "rhythm of formation." If we want to take personal spiritual formation seriously, we must plan for it. Contrary to popular belief, the Christian life doesn't just grow spontaneously. The seeds of the Spirit are sown into our hearts immediately upon faith, but it is tending to the soil of our spiritual formation that allows a vibrant Christian life to blossom. I believe a rule of life helps with this. While I often recommend books such as *The Common Rule* or *Habits of the Household* by Justin Earley and *Liturgy of the Ordinary* by Tish Warren Harrison, here are the four basic elements to consider when crafting a rule of life.

First, begin small by choosing a period of thirty days. This gives you a trial run of sorts. This test period gives you time to make some mistakes, get used to a new rhythm, and adjust expectations. If you can cultivate a rule of life for a month, you can do it for two months then six months and so forth. I would also recommend reviewing your rule of life every six months or so and assessing if it's working well with any new job responsibilities, family obligations, etc.

> The seeds of the Spirit are sown into our hearts immediately upon faith, but it is tending to the soil of our spiritual formation that allows a vibrant Christian life to blossom.

Second, pick a fruit of the Spirit that you wish to further cultivate for the current season you are in. Take time to read through Galatians 5:16–26, reminding yourself of what life in the Spirit looks like. As I'm writing this, the fruit of the Spirit I'm seeking to cultivate more is "gentleness." So, this is the first thing I wrote down at the beginning of the year on my rule. Every six months to a year when I reassess my rule, I decide whether I wish to continue focusing on this fruit or move to another.

Third, write out the days of the week (I start with Sunday) and put periods of "AM," "Lunch," and "PM." You can get more specific with times depending on your preference. For my rule, I like to keep the time periods a little more general. Take a moment to think through your week and jot down the events or items that are immovable (as in "Drop Off Kids at School," "Weekly Team Meeting," etc.). Next, I write down, in generic terms, the Bible reading and prayer times of my week. In the "AM" column, I write "M'Cheyne Plan Reading," in the "PM" column I write "Psalms and Proverbs," and in one or two "Lunch" time slots I write "Fast and Pray." I do my best to keep these slots consistent and schedule other things around them. If I know I want to fast on a Wednesday, I try to schedule lunch with someone on another day. If that can't happen for whatever reason, then I'll adjust my rule to compensate. The last thing I do when writing out the basic schedule is to add important family spiritual events. Specifically, this means local church worship, small group meetings, and family planning meetings. Most of these occur on Sundays for us. While it may be assumed in your schedule, it's important to write them down as a reminder of their importance. Sunday evenings we review our upcoming week's events, and increasingly, I want this to be an opportunity to pray and bring those things to the Lord. So, it needs to be on the rule.

Fourth, take each day's activities as you have laid them out and attach a verse or passage of Scripture to it. Verify its importance via Scripture. You don't have to make any weird interpretations, simply do your best to connect all your day to the Bible. For example, if you have a planned fast, write down Matthew 6:16–18 beside it. If you are having a church family over for dinner, remind yourself of the command to be hospitable in 1 Peter 4:9.

One final practical note: you can impose your rule of life on an already existing calendar or planner. Whether digital or hard copy, you can easily weave these aspects of your personal formation into what you are already doing. While you can create a separate document or planner, there is no need to throw out what already works for you. Just remember that the hope is to see your life and experience as shaped by your engagement with God. Start with God and his Word first, then add in activities and life plans accordingly.

Final Thoughts

Whether this is the first time for you to embark upon personal formation, or if you have been faithfully practicing personal disciplines for years, I hope that you feel both encouraged and challenged. Even if you have stalled out, having begun a reading plan or rule of life only to let it fizzle, don't give up. You can pick up where you left off or renegotiate your personal formation plan and start afresh. Like corporate formation, personal formation must be saturated with God's Word. Through Bible intake, we seek to permeate Scripture all throughout our experience. Whether reading, studying, or meditating, Scripture is meant to be the lifeblood of every Christian's heart. Connected to Scripture is our life of prayer and fasting. All three—intake, prayer, and fasting—are meant to flow into and out of one another in a seamless way. A life of spiritual disciplines is a beautiful life because it brings one ever closer to the heart of God. Never divorced from the corporate aspects of formation, Christians practice spiritual disciplines to complement their life in community. Additionally, personal formation is not spontaneous but planned. We must train, or discipline, ourselves for godliness (1 Tim. 4:7). Therefore, crafting a rule of life or something similar may help ensure that our spiritual growth takes place in a consistent and purposeful manner. A life of formation, both corporately and personally, requires effort. This effort is grace-driven and mercy-filled, empowered by the Spirit and undergirded by the person and work of Jesus Christ. Our efforts are not for the purpose of seeking rewards but, rather, living out of the rewards we have already received.

> **Whether reading, studying, or meditating, Scripture is meant to be the lifeblood of every Christian's heart.**

Resources for Further Study

Justin Whitmel Earley. *The Common Rule: Habits of Purpose for an Age of Distraction.* Downers Grove, IL: IVP Books, 2019.

Mason King. *A Short Guide to Spiritual Disciplines: How to Become a Healthy Christian.* Nashville, TN: B&H Books, 2023.

David Mathis. *Habits of Grace: Enjoying Jesus Through the Spiritual Disciplines.* Wheaton, IL: Crossway, 2016.

Donald S. Whitney. *Spiritual Disciplines for the Christian Life.* Revised and updated. Colorado Springs, CO: NavPress, 2014.

Dallas Willard, *The Spirit of the Disciplines: Understanding How God Changes Lives.* New York, NY: HarperOne, 1990.

Questions for Reflection

1. Reflect on your experience of spiritual disciplines in the past. Can you recall a season of dryness or a season of fruitful practice of disciplines? How did each of these feel?

2. What makes the practice of personal disciplines difficult generally? For you personally?

3. What practice of Bible intake is the easiest for you, as well as the most difficult? Why is this the case?

4. What has been your experience of fasting in personal formation? What are ways that you can begin, or continue, to emphasize the practice of fasting?

5. Have you ever created a rule of life or something similar? If so, take a moment to review it and assess how it is working in your personal formation. If not, start by rereading the section in this chapter on the rule of life and start making small steps toward creating one.

CHAPTER 7

Formation and a Life of Humility

> Do nothing out of selfish ambition or conceit,
> but in humility consider others as more
> important than yourselves.
> —Philippians 2:3

> The first way of truth is humility, the second way is
> humility, and the third way is humility.
> —Augustine of Hippo

William Law, an Anglican priest in the eighteenth century, wrote: "Let every day, therefore, be a day of humility; condescend to all the weaknesses and infirmities of your fellow-creatures . . . and condescend to do the lowest offices to the lowest of mankind."[1] Biblical figures, Christian thinkers,

---

1. William Law, *A Serious Call to a Devout and Holy Life* (Grand Rapids, MI: Christian Classics Ethereal Library), 169.

and everyday Christians throughout the centuries have learned that the only proper response to encountering God is humility. The fruit of humility is a complete distrust in oneself and recognition of one's inadequacies in the face of the infinite God. Humility is central to a life of spiritual growth. If humility is such a pivotal virtue, why is it missing from much of our discussions on Christian spiritual formation?[2] Regrettably, church leadership culture has inherited a paradigm where humility is not valued, ambition (often at the expense of others) is prized, and charismatic authoritarianism are the characteristics which make an effective leader. These leadership types may "get results," but often at the expense of destroying trust in the pastoral office and even causing much harm and abuse as a result. Yelling from the pulpit, espousing underhanded comments about another staff member's performance, and an ungodly smugness have for too long reigned in conference venues and preacher's lecterns.

> The fruit of humility is a complete distrust in oneself and recognition of one's inadequacies in the face of the infinite God. Humility is central to a life of spiritual growth.

Now, I am not saying that leaders are not called to exert authority, nor am I saying that

---

2. There are several individual works on humility, and some will be discussed in this chapter, but a brief survey of literature on Christian spiritual formation reveals a concerning lack of discussion on humility.

church leaders can't and shouldn't at times ruffle a few feathers. This must happen to be an effective pastoral leader. But the best pastors, at least the ones I've been privileged to be under and work alongside, know that their authority and "feather ruffling-ness" comes from God's Word, the penetrating truth of the gospel, and their sincere desire to speak truth in love. They also understand that their calling is one of service not severity. All Christ-followers are called to submit to the authority of God's Word, walking in humility while running

> **True Christian formation begins and ends with humility.**

from pride. In this chapter you will discover why humility is imperative for spiritual formation. To do this, I want to provide some examples from church history as well as help us understand why humility is so countercultural—even within the church. If we wish to experience the beauty of the Lord, then we must walk in humility.

The Forgotten Christian Virtue

Humility is tricky. For us to possess humility, we must simultaneously deny that we have it. As C. S. Lewis quipped: "If you think you are not conceited, it means you are very conceited indeed."[3] We are never as humble as we should be, but we are called to cultivate humility by submitting to the Lord

---

3. C. S. Lewis, *Mere Christianity* (New York, NY: HarperOne, 2015), 128.

and his Word, finding accountability with fellow believers, and asking the Holy Spirit to reveal our pride and arrogance. When humility escapes us, we look to the humble Savior who models obedience to God and a life of humility. Paul says that this type of "mind" belongs to all those who are in Christ Jesus. Paul calls the church to "do nothing out of selfish ambition or conceit, but in humility consider others as more important than yourselves" (Phil. 2:3). Is there any greater threat to godliness than selfish ambition and conceit? Is there anything harder than to consider others as more important than yourself? This is the difficult aspect of the Christian life and thus one of the greatest goals of spiritual formation. As James tells us: "God resists the proud but gives grace to the humble" (James 4:6). To be formed into the image of Christ is to be formed through humility.

> To be formed into the image of Christ is to be formed through humility.

Like oil and water, godly living and pride do not mix. Yet here is the weird part. Christians continue to platform and put forward ministry leaders based on worldly characteristics of success, charisma, and prestige. We're getting mixed messages in the church as to what ministry success looks like. Should leaders live humbly and serve others, or should they build a platform and accumulate power? I am not suggesting that every leader who has a large church, a sizable ministry budget, and successful book sales is being disobedient or arrogant. I trust that God has gifted such individuals for kingdom service and will require much of them based on that gifting. But this is the exception that proves the rule. Such leaders need to pursue humility, perhaps more than others, to live a godly life and move forward in their formation. But whether in a church of ten or ten thousand, the sin of pride can capture any heart. Humility is required of us all, whether in church ministry or not. So, if humility is what God requires, how is it accomplished? I don't have seven secrets to more humble living, but I want to present some historical examples for us to consider. I will then conclude with some observations to help us understand the ongoing importance of humility in Christian spiritual formation. But before moving forward, let me address a modern issue impeding our practice of humility.

Humility vs. Honor and Shame

There is a major issue infiltrating the church today with the potential to stifle humility and inhibit our spiritual formation. While it might be more prevalent on social media, this issue haunts the halls of many of our churches today. Many of our churches run on the fuel of honor and shame. Honor and shame cultures are prevalent in ancient and non-Western societies. Honor and shame cultures create an atmosphere of obligation and hierarchy, with numerous maneuvers and gestures necessary to maintain a right standing in society.

I think of the animated Disney movie *Mulan*. Mulan, a young woman in ancient China, wants to protect her aging father from having to fight in war. At one point in the movie, she steps forward to confront the emperor's messenger who had arrived at their village to conscript soldiers for the army.

When her father's name is called, she bursts forth begging the royal representatives to reconsider. Upon being rebuked for talking out of turn, her father warns her that she is dishonoring him. She then decides to conceal her identity by posing as a man and joins the army in her father's place. The entire movie revolves around her concealed identity and the possibility of bringing severe shame upon herself and her family. If she were to be found out, she could be executed. In true Disney fashion, all ends well as she is honored by the emperor for her bravery, regardless of being a woman. While this version may be somewhat Westernized, it's a helpful portrait of the dynamics of honor and shame.

In honor and shame cultures, humility is seen as weakness. The purpose is to maintain honor and power, not lose it. Humility means you desire to let go of honor and power for the sake of another. Those in an honor and shame culture must never choose to submit due to the perceived cost to one's social standing. Though more prevalent in non-Western societies, honor and shame is the essence of our modern cancel culture today. *Merriam-Webster* defines cancel culture as "the practice or tendency of engaging in mass canceling as a way of expressing disapproval and exerting social pressure."[4] If someone does not operate in the prescribed norms of society, then you have the opportunity and obligation to "cancel" them by not considering their thoughts or existence as valid. Conform your thoughts and actions to this kind of culture, and you will receive high praise and honor. Speak or act against

---

4. *Merriam-Webster.com Dictionary*, s.v. "cancel culture," accessed July 26, 2022, https://www.merriam-webster.com/dictionary/cancel%20culture.

the prevailing social norms, and you will be shamed out of existence.

Honor and shame cultures, and their modern equivalent of cancel culture, are completely contrary to the spirit of Christ and his incarnation. Christ set the standard for humble living when "he emptied himself by assuming the form of a servant, taking on the likeness of humanity" (Phil. 2:7). He put aside all the rights and honors owed to him as God for the sake of humbling himself "by becoming obedient to the point of death—even to death on a cross" (v. 8). Commentator G. Walter Hansen notes: "His submission to humiliation could be explained only as being the result of his own active obedience. He chose to be submissive as a slave rather than to be sovereign as the Lord."[5] While Christ's incarnation has cosmic ramifications, it also sets the bar for our life of humility. An act that appeared to produce the most shame—namely, putting aside divinity for a life leading to the cross—resulted in the highest honor. This honor is no fading worldly honor, but honor that results in every knee bowing and every tongue confessing "that Jesus Christ is Lord, to the glory of God the Father" (vv. 10–11). Our practice of humility is a participation in the humility of the Lord, with the goal of glorifying God and proclaiming the name of Jesus Christ. If we just understood that "success" in spiritual formation comes through humility, rather than through pride and arrogance, I believe we would see much more fruit produced for God's kingdom.

---

5. G. Walter Hansen, *The Letter to the Philippians*, The Pillar New Testament Commentary (Grand Rapids, MI: Wm B. Eerdmans, 2009), 156.

Humility is also learned through examples. While only Christ was perfectly humble, many Christians have reflected on humility throughout the centuries. I want to focus on just a few examples in church history so that we might once again understand its importance for Christian spirituality today.

A Short History of Humility

The beginning of our tour on the history of humility begins with a church father in the fourth century. Basil of Caesarea (ca. 330–379) was a church leader and theologian during a crucial moment in church history. Among other things, he ensured the continuation of orthodox Trinitarianism when many were questioning whether Jesus or the Holy Spirit were God. He was well-educated and well-connected, yet he ultimately submitted to the call of ministry. Not only did he write on grand theological topics, but he also helped reform and shape monastic Christianity. His thoughts contributed to Christian theology and spirituality in significant ways. He also consistently advocated for humility as central to Christian living. Church historian Michael Haykin notes: "A key area in Basil's thinking about monastic and episcopal leadership was the responsibility of the monastic leader and bishop to be a man marked by humility."[6] In one of his homilies, Basil declared: "For the soul grows like what it pursues, and is

---

6. Michael A. G. Haykin, *Rediscovering the Church Fathers: Who They Were and How They Shaped the Church* (Wheaton, IL: Crossway, 2009), 111.

molded and shaped according to what it does."⁷ The soul that pursues humble living and thinking grows in humility. The supreme model for humility is Christ. Basil asserted: "[We] find that everything the Lord did is a lesson in humility."⁸ Along with imitating Christ, Basil also advocated for imitating the apostles and other church leaders who exhibited humility. Basil exhorted his readers: "[Let] us imitate them, so that out of our humility there may arise for us everlasting glory, the perfect and true gift of Christ."⁹ When it comes to performing Christian virtue, humility is the door to the stage. Once inside, imitation of those who have come before becomes the way in which one properly practices virtue. Basil said: "[Strive] after humility in such a way that you come to love it. Love it and it will glorify you. In this way you will travel the good road leading to glory—that true glory which is found among the angels and with God."¹⁰ For Basil, only humility can produce excellence of character and true happiness because it has Christ as its foundation and life with God as its ultimate end.

Moving into the medieval era of the church, the virtue of humility remained a priority for Christian spirituality. In particular, the monastic reformer Bernard of Clairvaux (ca. 1090–1153) emphasized the role of humility as central to vibrant Christian living. So essential was humility to Bernard

---

7. Basil of Caesarea, "On Humility" 20.7 in Saint Basil the Great, *On Christian Doctrine and Practice*, Popular Patristics Series 47, trans. Mark DelCogliano (Yonkers, NY: St Vladimir's Seminary Press, 2013), 117.

8. Basil of Caesarea, "On Humility," 20.6, 116.

9. Basil of Caesarea, "On Humility," 20.6, 117.

10. Basil of Caesarea, "On Humility," 20.7, 119.

that he dedicated an entire treatise to the subject. In *The Steps of Humility and Pride*, Bernard advocated for the need to live lowly to rise spiritually. His work harkens back to the *Rule of St. Benedict*, a monastic manual authored by the father of Western monasticism, Benedict of Nursia (480–547). Like Basil, Bernard rooted the call for humility in the example of Christ. He stated: "The work of his tender love had its beginning in his eternal mercy, its completion in the mercy shown in his humanity."[11] Echoing Paul in Philippians 2, Bernard affirmed that Christ's incarnation was the ultimate show of humility. To know the truth, according to Bernard, is to know Christ and imitate his humility. *Steps* is more of a commentary on pride, but if one knows how to avoid pride then they will naturally pursue humility according to Bernard. At the end of his writing he confessed: "I could not very well describe the way up because I am more used to falling down than to climbing."[12] Certain attributes lead to increasing pride such as curiosity, boasting, and the habit of sinning. Submitting these desires to the Lord will increase humility. When we grasp a love for sin and make sinning a habit "the fear of God has been lost, replaced by contempt."[13] Thus, we need to be watchful against self-conceit and self-justification according to Bernard. These traits diminish humility and cause us to fall further from the truth of Christ.

---

11. Bernard of Clairvaux, *The Steps of Humility and Pride*, Cistercian Fathers Series 13A (Trappist, KY: Cistercian Publications, 1973), 40.

12. Bernard of Clairvaux, *The Steps of Humility and Pride*, 82.

13. Bernard of Clairvaux, *The Steps of Humility and Pride*, 78.

Protestant Reformers in the sixteenth century continued to value the virtue of humility. In particular, the French Reformer John Calvin (1509–64) wrote of its relevance to Christian spirituality. Speaking to the sin of pride and ingratitude, Calvin encouraged his readers: "By constant recognition of our vices, let us return to humility. By so doing, there will be nothing left in us to puff us up, but, on the contrary, there will be much to put us in our place."[14] Humility allows us to see our sin for what it is—contrary to godliness. Calvin understood that God sometimes allowed his people to experience suffering. The proper response to suffering is reliance upon God. Calvin noted: "Thus humbled, we learn to call on His strength, which alone can make us stand under the weight of such affliction. Indeed, the holiest among us know they stand by God's grace and not by their own virtues."[15] When we entertain thoughts of self-sufficiency, we should quickly turn to the cross for proper perspective. Calvin asserted that the cross "destroys the false notion of our own strength that we've dared to entertain, and it destroys that hypocrisy in which we have taken refuge and pleasure."[16] Only when we humble ourselves and submit to God will we "be stripped of our blind self-love and thus to be made aware of our own weakness."[17] Only by looking to the mercy and grace of God in Christ will we grow in humility according to Calvin. When we do so, we

---

14. John Calvin, *A Little Book on the Christian Life*, trans. and eds. Aaron Clay Denlinger and Burk Parsons (Orlando, FL: Reformation Trust Publishing, 2017), 34.

15. Calvin, *A Little Book on the Christian Life,* 61.

16. Calvin, *A Little Book on the Christian Life*, 63.

17. Calvin, *A Little Book on the Christian Life,* 63.

will most assuredly "experience the presence of divine power in which there is sufficient and abundant help."[18]

A couple hundred years after Calvin, the early American theologian Jonathan Edwards (1703–58) also encouraged the virtue of humility for Christian spirituality. Edwards ministered in the context of revivals which took place within the movement which has come to be known as the First Great Awakening in both England and colonial America. As other ministers heard of these revivals, they sought Edwards's advice on how to replicate what he was doing. Edwards dismissed any attempt to fabricate revivals and, instead, focused upon the sovereignty of God to bring about the spiritual awakening he witnessed. He also advocated for humility for spiritual renewal to take place. For Edwards, understanding pride and humility was not just theoretical, it was deeply personal. Edwards, in his "Personal Narrative," reflecting on the pride of his youth, recognized its presence even in maturity: "And yet I am greatly afflicted with a proud and self-righteous spirit; much more sensibly, than I used to be formerly. I see that serpent rising and putting forth its head, continually, everywhere, all around me."[19]

Edwards believed that one's conversion was wrapped up in their contemplation and rapture of God's beauty, rather than a consuming focus on the fruits of their spiritual transformation. With salvation came a holy disinterest in the things of the self, and a preoccupation of the things of God. A fruit

---

18. Calvin, *A Little Book on the Christian Life*, 62.
19. Jonathan Edwards, "Personal Narrative," in *Works of Jonathan Edwards*, 16:803.

of this salvation was love and humility. Surrender to the things of God required humility, and ongoing growth necessitated humility. For Edwards, no possibility of spiritual renewal existed without humility. Pride is the antithesis of spiritual renewal; only humility brings about true spirituality and growth. Spiritual pride is thus "the main door, by which the Devil comes into the hearts of those that are zealous for the advancement of religion."[20] Those who believe themselves to be closest to God are those who need most caution in regard to spiritual pride. Edwards advocated for "pure Christian humility" and compared its fruits with the fruits of spiritual pride.[21] The main attribute of humility is the suspicion of one's own heart rather than pointing out faults of others. Edwards noted: "Nothing sets a person so much out of the Devil's reach as humility, and so prepares the mind for true divine light, without darkness, and so clears the eye to look on things as they truly are."[22]

> **Pride is the antithesis of spiritual renewal; only humility brings about true spirituality and growth.**

Our short tour on the history of humility ends with J. I. Packer (1926–2020). Packer was an influential thinker and

---

20. Jonathan Edwards, "Some Thoughts Concerning Present Revival," in *Works of Jonathan Edwards*, 4:414.

21. Edwards, "Some Thoughts Concerning Present Revival," in *Works of Jonathan Edwards*, 4:418.

22. Edwards, "Some Thoughts Concerning Present Revival," in *Works of Jonathan Edwards*, 4:414–5.

writer within evangelicalism, his best-known work being *Knowing God*. Both in his writings and his life, Packer was a model of humility. In his work *Weakness is the Way*, Packer described the need for weakness and humility in the Christian life, prescribing a threefold way for how we are to cultivate humility. Packer saw weakness as a chosen state, recognizing that, regarding spiritual things, we are ultimately incapable. Packer stated: "The way of true spiritual strength, leading to real fruitfulness in Christian life and service, is the humble, self-distrustful way of consciously recognized weakness in spiritual things."[23] When we consider that we truly need God for every part of our spiritual life, it should lead to less contempt and more humility. Reflecting on Paul's words in 2 Corinthians 12:8–9, Packer affirms that "[God's] power is perfected in weakness" and, thus, whatever challenges lay ahead for us are opportunities to trust and lean upon God more fully.

When it comes to consciously cultivating the virtue of humility in one's life, Packer provided three postures to consider. The first is to *look to* Christ "as your loving Sin-Bearer and living Lord."[24] A constant looking to Christ melts away bitterness and self-entitlement and affirms your status as a disciple who is loved and cherished by God. The second posture is to *love* Christ "in unending gratitude for his unending love to you."[25] When we focus our heart on loving Christ, and

---

23. J. I. Packer, *Weakness Is the Way* (Wheaton, IL: Crossway, 2013), 16.

24. Packer, *Weakness Is the Way*, 50.

25. Packer, *Weakness Is the Way*, 51.

remember his unfading love for his people, then our desire for approval from others begins to fade. We then more earnestly serve the Lord rather than our own interests. Finally, Packer tells us to *lean* upon Christ. God told Paul that his grace was "sufficient" (2 Cor. 12:9), prompting Paul to lean upon God rather than his own strength. When we lean upon Christ we also "rely on him to supply through the Holy Spirit all the strength [we] need for his service, no matter how weak unhappy circumstances and unfriendly people may be making [us] feel at present."[26] We are to look to lean upon Christ now, because we will be living with Christ for eternity. Packer reminds us that we have future glories to come, which inform and guide our present-day faithfulness to Christ. If we want to see God's power manifested in and through us, then truly weakness is the way.

There are numerous more examples of humility in the Christian life, and many other writings on the subject. This survey was simply to show how figures throughout church history considered humility as vital for Christian spirituality. Any process of formation that neglects the ongoing need for humility is not Christian. Humility is the virtue that marks out the Christian life from any other spirituality. While others may peddle in humility; only in Christ does humility have meaning and purpose. Humility in Christian perspective removes the focus off ourselves and onto the beauty of God and the work of Christ. Humility informs everything from our corporate to our personal formation and is the only appropriate posture when we consider the majesty of the triune God,

---

26. Packer, *Weakness Is the Way*, 51.

our identity in Christ, and the work of the Spirit through us. Humility truly touches every aspect of our formation, start to finish. Let me turn now to consider some ways that humility should practically impact our journey of spiritual formation.

Humility in Practice

As I argued in chapter 6, what we do in our personal formation is modeled by and flows from our practices of corporate formation. The same is true for our practice of humility. We must seek to practice and model humility in relationship to others. This looks like imitating Christ in his submission to the Father's will (see John 6:38). We mutually submit to one another out of fear and reverence for Christ (see Eph. 5:21). This also means that we desire to practice restorative discipline. When sinned against, we should not wait for the person to own up and come to us for forgiveness; we go to them to seek reconciliation (see Matt. 18:15). We also seek to be accountable to one another. This means giving encouragement as well as receiving correction from others. Humble living desires to be open before others, speaking truth in love so we would collectively "grow in every way into him who is the head—Christ" (Eph. 4:15).

These postures flow both from the person and work of Christ and the inner life of the Trinity. In the Godhead there is mutual love and honor. There is no power struggle in the Trinity. There is no one-upmanship. To be formed in Christ's image is to practice humility for the sake of a flourishing and vibrant community akin to the inner life of God. Whatever Peter means by participating in the "divine nature," surely this is one aspect of it (see 2 Pet. 1:4). When practiced and increasing, humility creates a safe and inviting atmosphere where those in the community live for the good of the other while abiding in the love of Christ together.

Humility can also be abused. An emphasis on humility and submission can be used to promote a personality or set of personalities in the church. Leaders who exempt themselves from the practice of humility often see it as everyone else's job to humble themselves. It can also be used to deny personhood, especially in women. Verses that speak to the submission of wives to husbands and women keeping silent in church cannot be interpreted as the total subjugation of women under men. There are specific contexts and ways that those verses should be interpreted; abuse is not one of them. God will not allow his Word to be used as a tool of abuse. Women are made in the image of God and have gifts to be used for Christ's kingdom and service. Anyone who uses the virtue of humility to force your submission to their ungodly authority is in line with Satan not Jesus. Men can fall prey to unhealthy cultures of humility as well, believing that humility is somehow contrary to biblical manhood. However, the most biblical man was also the humblest man.

It's also important that the way of humility may never lead to popularity or "name recognition." For those who have gained popularity, however we might define that, the need for humility is even greater. As Jesus grew in popularity, he purposely withdrew by himself or with his closest disciples. At times, he taught in such a way as to disperse crowds, not attract them. So even if you gain notoriety, humility demands that you continue speaking what is true and attending to the state of your own soul. So especially for leaders in the church, you are a servant called to serve as you follow the One who came to serve (see Matt. 20:28). Serve the church because it's right and you love the people. If you minister only to gain influence, you will never earn people's trust. Influence will come over time as you model a life of love and humility. True ministry success is never gained through power-grabbing and manipulation. Remember that your Savior "who, existing in the form of God, did not consider equality with God as something to be exploited" (Phil. 2:6). Likewise, you should not count ministry position and authority as something to be exploited, but as a stewardship reflecting the heart of Christ for your people.

Final Thoughts

The nineteenth- and early-twentieth-century Dutch Reformed pastor Andrew Murray once confessed: "When I look back on my own religious experience, or on the church of Christ in the world, I stand amazed at how little humility is desired as the distinguishing feature of the discipleship of Jesus."[27] Like Murray, I recognize within both the church and my own soul the lack of humility as the distinguishing feature of my discipleship. While we may not deny the role of humility in spiritual formation, my concern is whether it is as explicit as it should be. Humility should be explicit and explicated to effectively accomplish the task of Christian

27. Andrew Murray, *Humility: The Beauty of Holiness* (Abbotsford, WI: Aneko Press, N.D.), Kindle loc. 40.

formation. At the end of the day, we cannot *mandate* humility, but we can *minister* humility, setting an example and providing encouragement for the practice of humility. The New Testament does not allow us to walk away with another view of Jesus Christ except as our Lord the humble Servant. Our world, and especially Christian ministry, affords us plenty of opportunity for pride and arrogance. For spiritual formation to be Christian, we should emphasize humility all throughout. We must not discuss humility for humanity's sake, but for the sake of our soul.

Resources for Further Study

Jerry Bridges. *The Blessing of Humility*. Colorado Springs, CO: NavPress, 2016.

Tim Keller. *Self-Forgetfulness: The Path to True Christian Joy*. Leyland, UK: 10Publishing, 2012.

Andrew Murray. *Humility*. Nashville, TN: B&H Books, 2017.

Dane Ortland. *Gentle and Lowly: The Heart of Christ for Sinners and Sufferers*. Wheaton, IL: Crossway, 2020.

J. I. Packer. *Weakness is the Way: Life with Christ Our Strength*. Wheaton, IL: Crossway, 2013.

Questions for Reflection

1. In what areas of your life do you see pride taking hold? Take time to confess and repent, asking the Lord to give you a greater spirit of humility.

2. What makes the pursuit of humility difficult? What cultural or personal barriers exist when it comes to aspiring toward a life of humility?

3. How is humility discussed in your church setting? What are ways it is emphasized? What are ways that it is neglected?

4. Reflecting on the life of Christ, what are three to five ways that Jesus exhibited humility?

5. Are there any ways in which honor and shame define your life and church experience more than humility? If so, what have been the effects on your spiritual life?

CHAPTER 8

Formation and the Pursuit of Friendship

"I have called you friends, because I have made known to
you everything I have heard from my Father."
—JOHN 15:15

You can only have close friends if you accept that you are
not your own but belong to Christ.
—ALAN NOBLE[1]

In the 2008 comedy *Step Brothers*, Brennan (played by Will
Ferrell) and Dale (played by John C. Reilly) are newly established stepsiblings after their single parents marry one another.
The movie shows the antics that ensue when two grown men
who have never left home are forced into sharing their lives

---

1. Alan Noble, "Friendship and Belonging in Middle Age," The
Gospel Coalition, April 27, 2022, https://www.thegospelcoalition.org
/article/friendship-middle-age/.

together. The goofy, and admittedly irreverent, tricks they play on one another come to a point when they discover that they have much more in common than they realized. Brennan asks: "Did we just become best friends?" "Yep," is Dale's quick and assured reply. Their friendship then develops through common interests such as velociraptors and Steven Seagal movies.

Friendship in this way is mostly about common interests. As long as there is agreement on favorite movies, fast-food restaurants, and '80s rock bands, friendship is possible. Common interests are certainly avenues for establishing relationships, but can true friendship be sustained on Taco Bell runs and the latest superhero movie franchise? Is it as simple as declaring someone as your best friend? I believe friendship goes deeper than what can be liked on a Facebook or Instagram feed. Friendship is the oxygen of our souls. It feeds us and sustains us in the best of times and the worst of times. It is the relationship that helps us walk through life's trials and life's joys. It can also be incredibly difficult to pursue and maintain. The church in a post-Christian society has a unique opportunity to prioritize and promote the role of friendship in our spiritual life. We live in a world at the mercy of false connections and fake friendships. Friendship has been devalued and defrauded. In a world with more possibilities than ever for connection, it's the very limitless possibility of connection that has depreciated meaningful friendships. The soil for cultivating fertile friendships has lost its vital nutrients.

Writer Alan O. Noble has observed why it seems so difficult to cultivate friendships in our age:

The way our lives are set up is broken. The
structures, habits, practices, and values. Our
city planning, markets, careers, laws, and
entertainment—all have been designed
with a false idea of what a human being is.
Collectively we assume that to be a human
is to belong only and ever to yourself. Thus,
friendships can be a nice perk of a successful
life, but friends can't demand anything of you
that you don't choose to give. At any point, if
a friendship is holding you back or bringing
you down, you can bail. Because the only person you owe happiness to is yourself.[2]

As we discussed in chapter 3 on union with Christ, our
current age sets a high priority on self-focused authenticity.
Friends in this sort of environment are helpful only if they
add to one's self-actualization. This, however, is not how
friendship has ever been conceived either philosophically, historically, or biblically. Friendship has always been integral to
mutual growth in virtue and as foundational for a flourishing
community. Friendship is for the other person just as much
as for oneself. In the Christian perspective, friendship is the
vehicle by which we grow in Christlike virtue and serves as
the foundation for a flourishing church community. In spiritual friendship, the mutual object of affection is God. We
also remember that Jesus Christ is our truest friend. Thus,
friendship is the way that we will truly flourish in our spiritual

2. Noble, "Friendship and Belonging in Middle Age."

formation. Without friendship, our spiritual formation—both personal and corporate—will be flat and fruitless. The question on everyone's mind is: How? If friendship is so vital, how come it is so hard to make and retain friends? Before we answer the *how* question, let's begin by exploring the *why* question of friendship.

The Need for Friendship

Some of you may be wondering if friendship is even the right category when discussing the Christian life and Christian spiritual formation. It seems that the Bible uses metaphors of the family as well as descriptions of fellowship more than friendship. After all, John said that "the one who loves God must also love his brother and sister," not his friend, right (see 1 John 4:21)? It is true that the metaphor of family is foundational to the way we describe our relationship to one another in the body of Christ. It is also true that the New Testament provides a broad image of fellowship when describing the church and its gathering together. Through Christ, we now have access to a loving and merciful Father, another sign of our familial connection (see Eph. 2:18). When discussing the role of friendship in Christian spirituality, however, we need to distinguish between *family*, *fellowship*, and *friendship*. The terms are not mutually exclusive. In fact, a thriving fellowship of love and service to one another provides the best pathway for Christian friendship to flourish. We need to build healthy biblical fellowship if we want to grow healthy biblical friendship. Jonathan Holmes describes biblical friendship as "fellowship that has been given added depth, refinement, and detail through active investment in one another's lives."[3] Healthy and thriving Christian fellowship leads to Christian friendship, a specific and localized relationship that flows from the heart of wider Christian fellowship. While healthy fellowship may draw us to a church, deep biblical friendships will keep us there. This is because friendship is what sustains us in life and allows us to persevere, giving us a place and space to share our needs and provide care for one another during life's trials.

In a sermon on friendship, Tim Keller lays out four principles of spiritual friendship that are helpful for us to consider, especially considering spiritual formation. We need to understand that friends are (1) needed, (2) discovered, (3) made, and (4) forever. Regarding the need for friendship, Keller observes: "[The ache for friendship] is one ache that is part of [Adam's] perfection. . . . God made us in such a way that we cannot enjoy paradise without friends."[4] The

> **In the Christian perspective, friendship is the vehicle by which we grow in Christlike virtue and serves as the foundation for a flourishing church community.**
> **In spiritual friendship, the mutual object of affection is God.**

3. Jonathan Holmes, *The Company We Keep: In Search of Biblical Friendship* (Minneapolis, MN: Cruciform Press, 2014), 18.

4. Timothy J. Keller, "Spiritual Friendship," Gospel in Life, March 1, 1998, https://gospelinlife.com/downloads/spiritual-friendship-6582/.

Creation account shows us man was created for a relationship with God and one another. Though man can have a certain kinship with animals, we can't share our soul with our golden-doodle. In this same sermon, expounding on the text of Acts 20:36–21:8, Keller observes the relationship between Paul and various friends in the text. Friends were essential to the gospel ministry of Paul and the other disciples. Keller notes: "To need and want deep friendships is not a sign of immaturity, but maturity. It's not a sign of weakness, but a sign of health."[5] We are made and built for friendship. Not only do we need people, but we also need to need people. As we explored in chapter 2 on the Trinity, our capacity and need for relationship is bound up in the creative genius of the triune God. Keller pointedly states: "The less you want friends, the less like God you are."[6]

The Discovery of Friendship

Once we realize that we need and are made for friendship, we need to start talking about how friendship is discovered. Like Brennan and Dale, it might take a long and arduous process of discovering commonalities. But unlike Brennan and Dale, Christians have a primary allegiance that unites and shapes our relationship with one another. Our identity in Christ is foundational for understanding ourselves and our relationship to Christ. It also means that we are united and in relationship with others who are in Christ. Whether a banker,

---

5. Keller, "Spiritual Friendship."
6. Keller, "Spiritual Friendship."

barista, or builder, all who are in Christ are one with each other. This does not automatically make us best friends, but it levels the playing field and gives us a starting point that is more meaningful and eternal than our favorite Premier League team. You may wear a suit and tie to church while I wear jeans and a T-shirt, but the only clothing that matters are our mutual robes of righteousness in Christ (see Isa. 61:10). The first component of our discovery of friendship is our mutual kinship in the Lord.

The second important discovery of friendship is the way in which the Lord has particularly knit each of us in covenant community with one another. Through Christ I have kinship with all Christians who claim the name of the Lord, but I have a particular commitment to a group of men and women in my local church. The "one anothers" of the New Testament have broad application across the community of Christ's followers, but they were originally written to apply to specific groups of men and women gathered in specific locations throughout the Roman Empire in the first century. They apply best today in the same way, to a localized gathering of men and women. I would argue that the "one anothers" make the most sense when we exist in a local church of Christ-followers committed to one another as potential and actual friends. This is part of our discovery.

When I consider my own local church, I see a diverse group of men and women from different ages, stages, and ethnicities. I count it a privilege to be among a people as diverse as our church body. Depending on the makeup of your church body, friendship may be easier or more difficult. When you look across the room on a Sunday morning, you may see people who look different than you. Everyone may be much older or younger. Perhaps everyone has a different socioeconomic status, family makeup, or ethnicity. It may even be a challenge for you to attend church for these reasons. I do not want to dismiss the struggles that come with finding meaningful connection in the local church. We are certainly more accustomed to finding friendship with those who look like us, dress like us, have the same interests as us, or any number of factors. But as a community we must first embrace that we are *already* connected to one another. The task now is to dive deeper into that connection and move toward making friendships.

The Making of Friendship

Friendship with one another begins in remembering our need for friendship. Friendship makes us more human, not less. We then move toward discovering that, as Christians, we have a foundation for friendship based on our mutual union with Christ as expressed in the local church. This doesn't automatically guarantee deep and lasting friendship, but this is the best place for us to start to move toward friend-making. Alan Noble observes: "Deep friendships require great sacrifice. They demand you set aside your preferences, goals, and hopes (at times) for the good of someone else."[7] Making friends means that we step out in faith and decide to invest the time necessary to grow in relationship with others. Within the church we often relegate this kind of activity to a Sunday school or small group ministry. This kind of ministry, I believe,

---

7. Noble, "Friendship and Belonging in Middle Age."

is necessary for growing relationships within the church. They do not, however, guarantee that such relationships will occur. The best Sunday school or small group still requires commitment from individuals to pursue relationships with one another for the sake of mutual growth in love for God and love for others. If we already know we need friendship, and we already know we have a common unity in Christ, then what is required for cultivation of friendship? One word: *time*.

While it may be that some friendships come more quickly than others, every single friendship requires time to grow. One study shows that it takes anywhere from 40 to 60 hours to go from an acquaintance to a casual friend, and then an additional 80 to 100 hours to grow from there.[8] Unsurprisingly, this study showed that friendship forms in places where we spend the most time, such as work, clubs, and religious groups. This alone is a good argument for consistent church participation as the mechanism for friendship formation. If you want to have friends, it might be as simple as putting in the time. That said, time investment must be matched with heart investment. The friendship odds are in your favor if you devote the time, but biblical friendship for the purpose of spiritual formation requires that we pursue the good of the other.

The good we are pursuing in spiritual friendship is the mutual love of God. There is one important fact to remember: we need to be committed to a friendship with God to grow in friendship with one another. Drew Hunter, in his book *Made*

---

8. See Jeffrey A. Hall, "How Many Hours Does It Take to Make a Friend?" *The Journal of Social and Personal Relationships* 36.4 (2019): 1278–96.

for Friendship, provides readers this exhortation: "In the end, the best advice for cultivating friendship is not to *find* a better friend but to *become* one."[9] The best way to become a better friend to others is to grow in your friendship with God. Through our union with Christ, each of us now has God as a friend. Jesus said that we now exist not as servants but as friends. We discussed cultivating this friendship with God in the chapters on corporate and personal means of grace. Individually we need to cultivate patterns and habits for experiencing God's grace and love, and our friendships with one another feed upon and contribute to our experience of God. Our desire to love the Lord works in tandem with our desire to love others. The best friends, however, are always setting their friendship with God as the priority. The beautiful part is that when we place our friendship with God as primary, we will see growth in friendship with others as a result.

Friendship Is Forever

In the song "Friends," singer and songwriter Michael W. Smith sings a very familiar chorus to any who lived through the contemporary Christian music culture of the 1980s and '90s. Whether the song brings back warm fuzzies or makes you cringe, the chorus truly communicates the essence of friendship in Christian perspective. It strikes a chord (no pun intended) in our hearts because it either communicates what

---

9. Drew Hunter, *Made for Friendship: The Relationship that Halves Our Sorrows and Doubles Our Joys* (Wheaton, IL: Crossway, 2018), 116; emphasis in original.

we know to be true, or what we wish to be true, about our friendships. For Christians, we need to remember that we are all indeed friends because of our shared union in Christ, yet we need to take the next step of solidifying friendship with one another. As we do, we must maintain the notion that these friendships are eternal. In fact, friendship is the relationship that will define us most in eternity.

When Jesus was confronted by the Sadducees in Matthew 22, they sought to back him into a theological corner regarding the nature of marriage and the resurrection. The Sadducees were proud of their supposed logical problem: In the resurrection, who would be the husband of a wife married seven times? Jesus's answer cuts straight to the heart: "You are mistaken, because you don't know the Scriptures or the power of God. For in the resurrection they neither marry nor are given in marriage but are like angels in heaven" (vv. 29–30). Jesus's answer exposed their pride and their denial of God's Word, and revealed the nature of God's people in the resurrection. Marriage will not be the defining relationship for God's people in the new heaven and new earth. This is not a devaluing of marriage and its design, but rather a revelation of what marriage is pointing toward. Marriage is a good yet temporary state. Our eternal destiny is to exist with one another in a new heaven and new earth in full relationship to God and one another, as friends. Truly, friends will be "forever if the Lord's the Lord of them."[10]

---

10. Michael W. Smith and Deborah D. Smith, "Friends," from the album *The Michael W. Smith Project*, 1983. Publisher: BMG

A practical implication of forever friendship is that we can and should begin cultivating that friendship now. Though we will have eternity to explore friendship with the multitude of saints, our eternal perspective on friendship should inform our practice of friendship in the present. Because we are bonded to one another in the Spirit, we should not neglect encouraging and exhorting one another toward faithfulness and holy living. Because we are members together in Christ's body, we should encourage the gifts and abilities we see in others. Because we "are all one in Christ" (Gal. 3:28), we can create an "everyone culture" in the church that values the contributions of others and honors them as fellow image-bearers of God.[11] And because we all kneel before Jesus as Lord, we should further encourage one another in our commitment to Christ and our growth in Christlikeness. These and related postures derive

> **Because we "are all one in Christ" (Gal. 3:28), we can create an "everyone culture" in the church that values the contributions of others and honors them as fellow image-bearers of God.**

Rights Management, Capitol Christian Music Group, Capitol CMG Publishing.

11. The idea of an "everyone culture," where everyone has gifts and abilities that need cultivation in order for any organization to thrive, comes from Robert Kegan and Lisa Laskow Lahey, *An Everyone Culture: Becoming a Deliberately Developmental Organization* (Boston, MA: Harvard Business Review Press, 2016).

from our commitment to one another as forever friends in Christ. Let's consider now some practical ways in which friendship connects to and fuels our spiritual formation.

Connecting Friendship to All of Life

In the 2022 survey "The Greatest Needs of Pastors," Lifeway Research asked several pastors to respond and share the greatest needs they have in ministry. The top five needs from a recent survey show the following:[12]

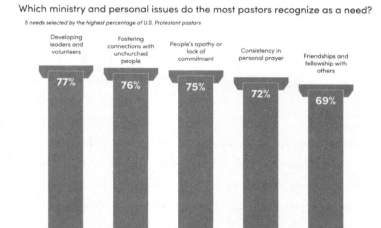

The Greatest
Needs of Pastors

Which ministry and personal issues do the most pastors recognize as a need?

5 needs selected by the highest percentage of U.S. Protestant pastors

Developing leaders and volunteers	Fostering connections with unchurched people	People's apathy or lack of commitment	Consistency in personal prayer	Friendships and fellowship with others
77%	76%	75%	72%	69%

Lifeway research   Source: Lifeway Research phone survey of 1,000 U.S. Protestant pastors conducted March 30–April 22, 2021

As you can see, the number-five greatest need is "friendship and fellowship with others." Pastors recognize this as a

---

12. "The Greatest Needs of Pastors," Lifeway Research, https://research.lifeway.com/greatestneeds/.

significant need, but I would argue that the other top needs identified would be greatly impacted if the number five need were being met. The key I believe for ministry leaders, and any Christian, is to see every day and every experience as an opportunity to pursue and cultivate friendship. What if we saw all of life as an opportunity to pursue friendship with others? Daryl Crouch elaborates on this point for pastors: "Friendship in ministry has its own set of challenges, but it's possible that pastors often have trouble developing friendships because we begin our relationships with other people thinking of them as future volunteers rather than as future friends."[13] Whether in pastoral ministry or in parent meetings, we can see every relationship as potential friendships. Our joy and satisfaction in work and life will increase when we take this relational approach. This may not sound good in a job interview when the interviewer asks why you want a particular job and you reply with something like, "I want to make friends," but functionally this is how we should operate.

> See every day and every experience as an opportunity to pursue and cultivate friendship.

Regarding spiritual formation, this helps us see every fellow Christian as a potential spiritual friend for the sake of

---

13. Daryl Crouch, "3 Uncommon Habits Pastors Need to Build Friendships," Lifeway Research, January 22, 2022, "https://research .lifeway.com/2022/01/26/3-uncommon-habits-pastors-need-to-build -friendships/.

mutual growth in Christlikeness. This does not mean we have to be besties with everyone in the church, but we shouldn't neglect the possibility that someone sitting in the pew in front of us is a new friendship to pursue. This also doesn't mean we view other Christians as a means to simply reach our personal spiritual goals. This is contrary to the spirit of Christian friendship. If friendship is for selfish gain, then friendship is a sham. Friendship is indeed a means to an end, but that end is mutual love for God. And since the love and beauty of God is inexhaustible, friends will never tire of helping one another explore the riches of God. Drew Hunter provides a helpful perspective here: "Friends do things together. It's not complicated. And the best part of friendship is not the *doing* but the *being*. When you're with good friends, just being together is more important than whatever it is you're doing."[14] Friends are comfortable simply being with one another, and for Christian friends, that will contribute to our growth.

Reminders for Cultivating Friendship

While the initial spark of friendship may happen quickly, remember that it takes time to cultivate meaningful friendship with one another. Good friendships do not happen instantaneously. Don't give into the "Instagramification" of friendship. We can't expect instant results. Be okay with little blocks of time that add up and slowly build as you grow in friendship. A walk here, a coffee there, a hug on a Sunday morning—all build toward and solidify relationships. A regular text message, call,

---

14. Hunter, *Made for Friendship*, 107; emphasis in original.

or meetup adds to our friendship investment account. Even in those seasons where friendship stalls, the accumulation of time and experience tips the scales of friendship toward eventual success. No one is as good a friend as they ought to be, but as we progressively pursue the good of the others and our mutual love of God, we are sharpened in our ability to be a better friend.

Hunter observes: "It's true that we enter friendship voluntarily. But once we enter it, is it also true that we don't have any responsibilities to our friends? No. Everyone expects loyalty from friends."[15] Remember, friendship requires commitment. We have to say yes to some things and no to others to prioritize friendship. We see this in the work of Christ in the Incarnation. Paul states that the Son said no to holding on to his divine rights and yes to taking on flesh and submitting himself to the point of death on the cross (see Phil. 2:5–8). To be a good friend and be fruitful in our formation, we need to say yes to the desires of the other while being willing to say no to ours. A life of sacrifice is synonymous with friendship. The beauty of spiritual friendship is that sacrifice reaps eternal reward, a greater affection for God and others. The beautiful mystery of the Christian life is that "whoever loses his life because of [Christ] will find it" (Matt. 16:25). In spiritual friendship we agree to lose our lives together for the sake of Christ and others, and in that we will find true pleasure and joy welling up and filling our soul.

This next reminder speaks to the life of discipleship more generally. Discipleship in Christian perspective is best

---

15. Hunter, *Made for Friendship*, 83.

understood as a life of friendship with God and others. We often think of discipleship as transactional or contractual. There are certainly times in our life as a disciple when we have "transactional" moments. When we sign up for a four-week class on spiritual disciplines, or attend a Christian conference, or engage in a time-bound Christian book club. All these good elements of Christian spirituality and growth can feel contractual by expecting to receive a benefit for your investment. But when Jesus called the Twelve, he invited them into his life. They witnessed him weep, they saw him get angry, they observed the compassion he showed others. They also benefited from his encouragement and exhortation. He called them friends and entrusted them with perpetuating the gospel mission (John 15:15; Matt. 28:19–20). He gave them space to be themselves, but also pressed them toward greater faith and trust in God. Jesus shows us what it means to be a friend and shows us that discipleship is an exercise in intimate friendship. To be a disciple of Christ is to be his friend. We must carry forth this spirit in every discipleship activity we embark upon.

A final reminder is not to give up on friendship even if you've been hurt in the past. Because of sin, we will all fail to be the friends we should be. Sometimes we will have people who claimed to be our friends, only to later find we were being used by them for some purpose. Others of us have been subject to ongoing manipulation by those who claimed to love us and have our best interests in mind. These are all tragic circumstances and undoubtedly pollute the way many of us have viewed friendship. If this is you, I would first encourage you to find solace in the one True Friend who never leaves or forsakes you and is continually interceding for you (see Heb. 7:25). For some, it may be beneficial to enter a professional counseling relationship where there is safety to share your experience and receive encouragement and wisdom.

At the end of the day, friendship is too important to forsake altogether. It may be slow, and ongoing healing may be necessary, but continue to pursue friendship for the sake of your soul and the good of the other. Alan Noble says, "There are no adequate substitutes for a kind look from a friend, or a sympathetic word, or the hard advice you need, or a reminder of Christ's love. We need to give and receive all these gestures of love because this is what we were fundamentally made for."[16] If you have been deeply wounded by friends and those whom you once trusted, I pray that you will find a space and a group of people to share your experience and find healing in the Lord. I hope that true and meaningful friendship will take root and blossom. There may be a season where you need to receive more than you can give in friendship, and that's okay. A true friend will understand and walk alongside you, pointing you to the grace and mercy of God and encouraging you to trust in the Lord's goodness. Mutually, you can move toward God as you move toward each other.

Final Thoughts

Tim Keller states: "The less you want friends, the less like God you are."[17] Friendship is important for the Christian life

---

16. Noble, "Friendship and Belonging in Middle Age."
17. Keller, "Spiritual Friendship."

because it makes us more like God; it's what God intended for us. The need for friendship makes us more human, not less. Regarding our spiritual formation, friendship is pivotal; without friendship, our formation is fruitless. Spiritual friendship is how we persevere in beholding God's beauty and friendship directs us to the means of our growth, God's Word. Friendship also reminds us of God's goodness in rescuing us from sin and reestablishing friendship with us. While friendship may require more than agreement on favorite dinosaurs and action movies, it can be as simple as asking someone: "Did we just become best friends?"

> **Friendship is important for the Christian life because it makes us more like God; it's what God intended for us.**

Christians have a unique opportunity in our culture to show the potential for true friendship in the church. In a culture where friendship is optional, Christians can show how it is integral to our true happiness and flourishing. Spiritual friendship cultivates love for God, which is the most satisfying thing in the world. When we discover that the life of formation and discipleship *is* the life of friendship, we will begin to find spiritual growth taking place in new and exciting ways. By seeing everyone as a potential friend we can begin good and fruitful conversations that may lead to enjoying true friendship in the light of God's grace and love.

Resources for Further Study

Victor Lee Austin. *Friendship: The Heart of Being Human.* Grand Rapids, MI: Baker Academic, 2020.

Jonathan Holmes. *The Company We Keep: In Search of Biblical Friendship.* Minneapolis, MN: Cruciform Press, 2014.

Christine Hoover. *Messy Beautiful Friendship: Finding and Nurturing Deep and Lasting Relationships.* Grand Rapids, MI: Baker Books, 2017.

Drew Hunter. *Made for Friendship: The Relationship that Halves Our Sorrows and Doubles Our Joys.* Wheaton, IL: Crossway, 2018.

Kelly Needham. *Friend-ish: Reclaiming Real Friendship in a Culture of Confusion.* Nashville, TN: Nelson Books, 2019.

Questions for Reflection

1. Take a moment to reflect on a past friendship, a current friendship, and someone who you may wish to pursue in friendship. Write down names and pray for those individuals, asking God to help you be a better friend to those people.

2. In what ways does understanding your relationship to God as one of friendship change the way you view your spiritual life?

3. What difference would it make in your life if you considered all your life activities as opportunities for friendship?

Write down people in those different places where you can cultivate friendship.

4. Does your church have a culture of healthy friendship? If so, what are the factors that contribute to this? If not, what do you think are the major roadblocks?

5. Take a moment to reflect and write down ways you can be a better spiritual friend to others. Which of those things can you begin practicing in order to be a better friend?

Conclusion

I end where I began, with Star Trek. This time, I want to focus on one of the greatest Star Trek films of all time: *Star Trek II: The Wrath of Khan*. Even if you haven't seen the movie, you probably recognize the iconic image of Captain Kirk screaming, "KHAAANN!" into his communicator, reverberating throughout space. The movie, which is a continuation of an episode from the original *Star Trek* television series, involves a villain named Khan Noonien Singh. Khan, a genetically modified tyrant from the late twentieth century who was cryogenically frozen before Captain Kirk and the crew of the *Enterprise* revived him, believed he was destined to rule. His compatriots were also of a genetically modified class of humans who were convinced of their own elite status. Khan's grudge against Kirk for unintentionally marooning them on a wasteland of a planet grew into rage and blind pride which eventually overtook him and led to his demise. Though Khan was eventually defeated by the heroism of Kirk and his crew, he left plenty of destruction in his wake, including the death of Spock, the infamous Vulcan and best friend of James Kirk. Believing his own press, Khan became a lethal brute only capable of hate. Only he knew the way forward, only he could have control, only he was competent to lead. His superior genes led to his annihilation. His pride was his downfall.

There is a potential Khan in all of us. We can either choose the path of pride and arrogance or humble submission. We can either see our position in God's family as an opportunity to grow in love for others or love for ourselves. We can choose to serve and walk alongside others with grace, or we can lead a life that will have someone screaming out our name in frustration ("COLLLLEEEEMAN!"). Like Khan, we can believe our own press, or we can believe what God's Word says about us and his plan. We can choose to behold God's beauty or our own. From our TV screens to our social media feeds, we are being formed to think and feel that we are the only person that matters. Thus, the mission and goal of Christian spiritual formation has never been more pressing. If we are to be formed into the image of Christ, we need the ministry of formation to be stronger now more than ever. Whether in a church of fifty or five thousand, we can't take our spiritual formation seriously enough. But I want to close with a final encouragement to those who think that a "formula for formation" is all we need.

Some of us really love using Excel spreadsheets. You love the thrill of inputting numbers, building formulas, and extracting accurate results. Whether budgeting for your home or calculating returns on corporate investments, these kinds of tools help us maintain order in our lives and society. We need spreadsheets and we need spreadsheet gurus. But the

Christian life is no spreadsheet. While there are tried-and-true spiritual formulas, our lives cannot be predicted with the accuracy of a mathematical equation. There is no one method of Christian spiritual formation.

The Christian life is more akin to a painting. While there is a certain order and form, each painting is different and unique. You do need to know some basics to embark upon any artistic endeavor, but each painting will be unique. Though brushstrokes may be similar, and color palettes match in various ways, the result will be different every time. The point is not the brand of oil pastels used. The significance is found in the completed work displaying the artist's craft and design. While artists require training, the method always serves to highlight the unique creations produced. The same is true for Christian spirituality and the kingdom of God. We must adhere to tried-and-true methods of formation, but the result must be different every time. Just as each image-bearer of God is unique, so are the outcomes of our spiritual formation. The goal for all of us is the same, but each of us will be a unique rendering of God's creative genius in his kingdom for all eternity. This is the spirit that underlies faithful Christian formation.

My hope for this book and for you is that you would not see formation as a mechanical process but as an opportunity to experience the beauty of God in your life and the life of the church. We should not think of spiritual formation like a factory, churning out the same widget every time. The idea of a factory has too long dominated our thinking regarding discipleship in the church. If you turn the right knobs and pull the right levers, you get a consistent result. I think a better word is *culture*. Are we participating in a culture of formation that takes seriously the doctrine and practice of the Christian faith? *Culture* is an important word, but it is also a flexible one. Every biblically-faithful church should have the same general characteristics, but they must look different based on context.

> We who have been welcomed into the life of God through his goodness and grace are all being shaped by his truth to behold his beauty more deeply.

We who have been welcomed into the life of God through his goodness and grace are all being shaped by his truth to behold his beauty more deeply. Yet this does not mean that we must all look the same. In fact, the biblical portrait of eternity speaks to the united yet unique people of God worshiping around the throne of God (see Rev. 7:9). Is your church more like a factory or a culture when it comes to discipleship and formation? Are you encouraged to be free in your identity with Christ, understanding that your freedom is meant to glorify God and serve others in love (see Gal. 5:13)?

If you are ready to embark for the first time on the journey of Christian formation, I hope you will see the foundations and practices provided here as beneficial. If this is not your first spiritual formation rodeo, I still pray you have grown in your appreciation and practice of formation through reading this book. For everyone, I hope you will gather a group of others in your local church to learn together what it means to practice more faithful spiritual formation corporately and individually. If you are a pastor or ministry leader, I hope this book challenges you to take seriously the role of good Christian formation in the context of the local church. If it's overwhelming for you, start small by introducing language of formation into your church's vocabulary. Begin by assessing how your worship either enhances, or disrupts, Christian formation. As you have influence and earn trust within your church, begin introducing practices outlined here and encouraging people to engage in personal disciplines. You can never go wrong with injecting your worship with more Scripture. You could also begin by hosting a study on personal spiritual disciplines and connecting those to the corporate worship in small yet significant ways. The hope is to move the needle of formation a little further. If this book has helped accomplish that, then I'm thrilled.

The final encouragement echoes what has been said in various other places here: do not fret if formation is slow. Our sanctification, and even building a culture of spiritual formation, cannot happen overnight. While some may be further along than others, everyone's growth is different. Nor should every church look alike, but as the Lord allows the opportunity, I pray your church will grow in its practices of corporate formation. There is no perfect church or perfect Christian, there is only one perfect Savior. Our goal is to be formed into his

> **You can never go wrong with injecting your worship with more Scripture.**

image, not the image of a church model or even the image of
this book. As the Spirit leads you and your church body, you
should follow. If you are walking humbly together, led by
God's Spirit through God's Word, then do not be ashamed to
practice formation in the way you feel led. I believe the encouragements provided in this book
are the essentials both doctrinally and practically. I don't
believe I have provided the final
word on formation nor solved
every formation problem you
may encounter. My prayer is
that through what has been presented here you will desire God
more fervently in your life and
be better equipped to behold his
beauty. Formation is the process
of image-bearers called by the goodness of God, shaped by the
truth of God, to behold the beauty of God. Forever. This book
and all books on formation will eventually pass away, but the
Lord remains. To this let me end with Augustine of Hippo in
his *Confessions*: "Lord God, grant us peace; for you have given
us all things, the peace of quietness, the peace of the sabbath,
a peace with no evening. This entire most beautiful order of
very good things will complete its course and then pass away;
for in them by creation there is both morning and evening."[18]

> **Formation is the
> process of image-
> bearers called by
> the goodness of
> God, shaped by
> the truth of God,
> to behold the
> beauty of God.**

---

18. Saint Augustine, *Confessions* 13.35.50 in *Confessions*, trans. Henry
Chadwick (New York, NY: Oxford University Press, 1998), 304.